HOW TO BE REAL MAN

THIS BOOK IS DEDICATED TO ALL THE REAL MEN I'VE KNOWN
- AND ALL THOSE YET TO COME

By Julian Clary
with Mark Leigh & Mike Lepine

BCA

This edition published in 1992 by BCA
by arrangement with Virgin Publishing Ltd.,
338 Ladbroke Grove, London, W10 5AH.

CN 6783

A catalogue record for this book is available from the British Library

Designed by Paul Elmes and John Gowers
Original photography by Sean Johnson and Peter Mountain
Additional photographs courtesy The Image Bank, Rex Features
Illustrations by Colin Hadley, Rian Hughes, Kevin Williamson
Cover design by Slatter-Anderson

Printed and bound in Great Britain by Varnicoat Ltd, Pershore, Worcestershire

INTRODUCTION

The human male comes in all shapes and sizes but can I, Julian Clary, renowned homosexual and glamorous celebrity, actually be from the same species as the Real Man? What accident of nature can account for this?

Who knows, but I've learnt to accept him. His pot belly, scuffed training shoes, permed hair and negligible intellect I find rather endearing. He can't help it, after all.

My jaw drops with fascination every time I see one. As a punter at one of my shows, he's a gift, a visually hilarious spectacle, ideal for a barrage of lewd remarks and with no brain to respond! I'm on to a winner every time.

So over the years I've come to know a Real Man when I see one. He may be at the other extreme on the scale of masculinity, but I can see, were it not for the social conditioning, the genetic gift of bone structure and cosmetics by Lancome, there but for the grace of God go I...

This book is essentially for men who are not quite 'Real'. They'd like to be, but somewhere along the line they've picked up that tell-tale smidgeon of sensitivity. They're too considerate, too polite, or just too thin.

Don't worry. All is not lost. The next 77 pages tell you everything you need to know, and if you're not a Real Man by the end of it, I'll eat my diamanté bum-bag.

love

Julian x

HOW TO BE THE SEXY, MAN OF MYSTERY TYPE

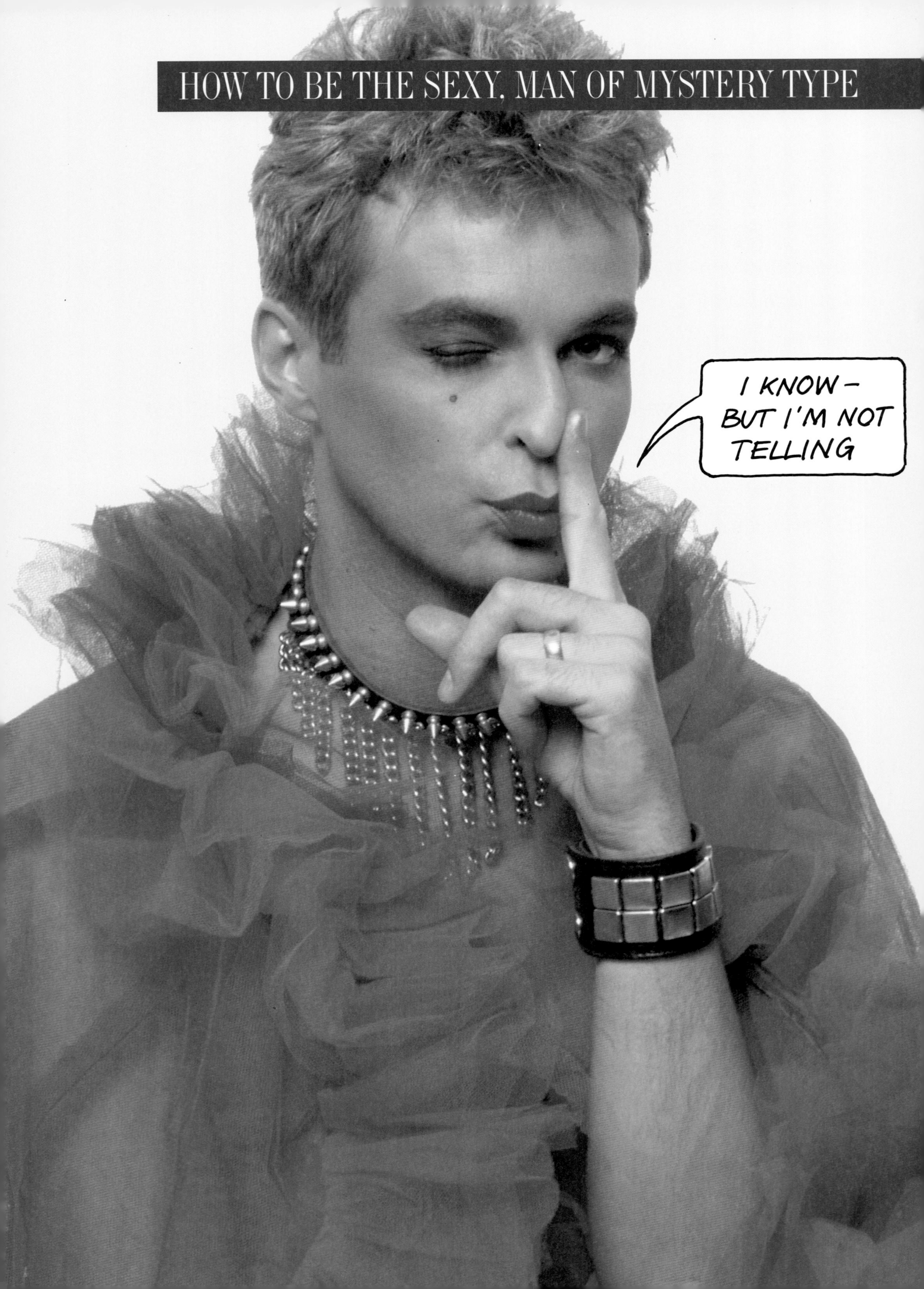

My First Year

MY NAME IS: WOODS STEVEN PEARCE KEOWN WALKER PLATT PALMER BATTY SINTON LINEKER SHEARER ENGLAND CRAPPY EUROPEAN CHAMPIONSHIP TEAM

I AM A LITTLE: ~~Boy~~ / Girl SOD

WHO I MOST RESEMBLED AT BIRTH: ~~Mum~~ / ~~Dad~~ THAT DICKHEAD FROM RIGHT SAID FRED

I WAS NAMED AFTER: MY DAD GOT PISSED

MY FIRST VISITOR: THE SOCIAL WORKER — BUT THEY COULDN'T PROVE NOTHING

MY FIRST TOYS: FLUFFY BUNNY, TALKING TEDDY BEAR, MULTI-COLOURED BUILDING BLOCKS — ALL NICKED FROM TIMMY HUTCHINGS WHEN I SHARED HIS PLAY PEN

MY FIRST STEPS: MY LEFT FOOT TO TIMMY HUTCHINGS' TESTICLES (OR WHERE HIS TESTICLES WOULD BE, WHEN THEY DROP)

MY FIRST SOLIDS: CHICKEN VINDALOO I TEETHED ON: 20 B+H

MY FIRST SENTENCE: WHO ARE YOU CALLIN' A BABY? STITCH THAT!

MY FIRST BOOK: REAL MEN ONLY, JULY 1992

MY EARLY AILMENTS: SPLIT LIP (12 TIMES), BRUISED KNUCKLES (18 TIMES), BLACK EYE (23 TIMES)

MY FIRST LITTLE GIRLFRIEND: SALLY JONES 18-13-18 WHAT A FIGURE!

MY FIRST SHOES: SIZE 1, 14-HOLE DM BOOTIES

MY FIRST MISCHIEF: STEALING A PEDAL CAR FROM PLAY GROUP AND RUNNING AWAY AFTER I CRASHED IT.

STARTING OUT IN LIFE AS A REAL BABY

NURSERY RHYMES FOR REAL LITTLE BOYS

Bar, Bar, Barman, have you any beer?
Yes mate, yes mate, there's loads here
Six pints for Darren
Eight for my mate Tone
And ten pints for me because I'm driving home.

The grand old Duke of York
He had 10,000 men
- Oh no. Sorry, I'm wrong.
I was thinking of his wife.

Videos blue, dilly, dilly
Videos sick
It's the vice squad, dilly, dilly
It's down to the nick...

Jack made Jill go on the Pill
They didn't want a baby
It failed that day
Jack ran away
She hasn't seen him lately.

BED TIME STORIES FOR REAL LITTLE BOYS

ALADDIN
...Then the voice bellowed, 'I am the Genie of the lamp and I am here to grant you three wishes.'

'In that case,' said Aladdin, 'I'll have all the Special Brew I can drink, a lifetime subscription to Club International *and a K-reg XR3i Cabriolet with alloy wheels and a tasty stereo.'*

And Aladdin lived happily ever after.

THE UGLY DUCKLING
...Then who should approach the sad little duckling but two handsome, proud swans.

The swans looked her up and down and saw that she wasn't like the other ducklings. The proudest swan turned to his partner and said, 'Don't fancy yours, mate!'

Then they wet themselves laughing and went off in search of some real talent. As for the duckling - well, life's a bitch...

THE THREE LITTLE PIGS
...Then the big bad wolf shouted, 'Come out, come out little piggies, or I'll huff and I'll puff and I'll blow your house down!'

The three little piggies in the straw house looked out the window and laughed, saying, 'We know you're a sixty-a-day man, Mr Wolf, and you haven't got the puff to blow even this crappy straw house down!'

But then Mr Wolf took out his packet of Marlboros...and his cigarette lighter... then set the straw house on fire and had a lovely spare rib barbecue.

LEARNING THROUGH PLAY

If you want your son to grow up to be a Real Boy, you'll need to think a little more carefully about the toys you let him have - do they glorify war, teach selfishness and contempt for those around him? If so, marvellous!

Here are some of my favourite Real Boy toys, designed to help your son get the start in life he needs...

JUNIOR TV REPAIRMAN

Fun and educational! Who knows, this could be the start of a promising trade! Includes set of screwdrivers, television repairman hat and a special booklet on 'How to fix it so that the TV breaks down again ten minutes after you've gone'.

'THE BILL' EMBROIDERY SET

Capture all the action and excitement of the smash hit Thames TV series with this fabulous embroidery set! Stitch the villains up a treat this weekend!

TERMINATOR 2 IRONING SET

I'll be back - and I expect my shirts to be neatly ironed! Don't disappoint the manhunting killer cyborg from the future. Do all your ironing on this neat 1/3rd scale junior ironing board with miniature working iron! Hasta la vista, scruffy appearance!

JUNIOR PLUMBER PLAYSET

Drive your parents 'round the bend' with this fun playset! Contains absolutely nothing (because plumbers never have what they need with them when they turn up).

JUNIOR FORD TRANSIT PEDAL VAN

Imagine it! Your own pedal action tradesman's van - just like Dad's! Have great adventures, cutting up other pedal cars, ignoring traffic lights, yelling abuse at other drivers and parking on the pavement - just like Dad!

Comes complete with indicators (non-functioning), 1970s tax disc, dodgy steering, choice of rude window stickers, offside dents and scrapes and filthy mattress in the back in case you get lucky.

STREET CAR™ JOYRIDER SET

Be just like your older brother with this fun toy car playset. Contains 1 x length of straight track, 1 x stolen vehicle, 1 x police pursuit vehicle, 1 x car containing family coming back from their holiday in the opposite direction.

JUNIOR JESUS™ PLAYSET

Disapprove of war toys? Give your child a positive role model! Bumper fun set includes robe, non-toxic, flame-retardant beard, stigmata rub-down transfers, plastic loaves and fishes, cardboard punch-out disciples, extra-safe foam 'crown of thorns' and polystyrene flip-flop sandals with special 'floating' action - walk across garden ponds, canals, disused gravel pits, anything! Everything a budding saviour could want.

THE REAL MAN NEXT DOOR

It's terribly suburban, I know, but I do look forward to people popping in without warning. There's something exciting about someone barging in when you least expect it. You know the sort of thing, to borrow a clothes peg or two, or just to have a chat over a coffee and a fudge finger.

Now I love gossip. Once I get my hands on some juicy tidbit my tongue never stops wagging. And there's plenty to wag about where I live. I see my bijou residence as a paradise isle in the middle of Real Man-infested waters. It must be extremely easy to be a Real Man Neighbour - after all, all the people living round me have managed it.
Let them be your inspiration...

No 5: The Clarke family. Eight-year-old Ricky is well on his way to becoming a Real Man. Last week he was sick 22 times all over my sweet peas. It's frightening how potent lemonade shandy and a Tizer chaser can be.

No 3: The Carters. Haven't seen Mr Carter since they showed his photo on *Crimewatch UK* last week. He looked a bit shifty, but I blame the lighting.

No 7: Jeff and Karen. They've got Sky TV and every Tuesday and Friday 48 of Jeff's mates come round, drink themselves silly watching live Bulgarian soccer and spend 45 minutes shouting 'See ya' when they leave at 2a.m. I don't mind at all. Sometimes, if I'm feeling frisky I call 'coo-ee' and give a cheery wave. They soon disperse then.

No 6: The O'Connell family. If you want to see what three or four unlit skips outside your house could look like, then this is the house for you.

No 11: The MacLeod family. Their two delightful teenage sons ring your bell at 3a.m. and stare through the peephole in your door wearing ski masks. I know it's them, though, because they always leave cottage cheese over my letterbox. Saucy lads.

No 13: Mrs Hughes. A dear little old lady who's dead but who's still there because her next-door neighbours don't realise that they haven't seen her for three months. Who's watering her tomato plants, though? That's what bothers me.

No 9: This is my humble abode, readers. The jewel in the crown of the estate. I'm just waiting for Loyd Grossman to come probing through my keyhole. Well, we can all dream. I don't know if you can see it in the photograph but I've got a diamanté door chain that's proven to be quite a talking point...

PAGE 7 HUNK

Cast your eyes over Julian. He's a real catch! Girls fall for him hook, line and sinker because, as you can see, he's no minnow in the tackle department. And don't worry about landing a few crabs - he always keeps his rod clean!

Part 1 of
JULIAN PULLS IT OFF

'CRIPES,' yelped Julian, Head Boy at St Gregory's, barely able to conceal his surprise. 'I've never seen one that big before!'

'Nor me,' yelped Tiny.

They both looked on aghast as Spotty Bates finished sliding the weapon out of the top of his trousers.

'I produced it in metalwork this morning and everyone was amazed. This was the only way I could smuggle it out,' Spotty explained.

'What an absolutely top hole weapon!' enthused Julian, taking the weight in his hands and admiring the perfect balance. 'It's super, Spotty! This will really come in handy. I just hope we don't have to use it.'

'I can't wait until lights out,' shrieked Tiny.

'Nor me!' responded Spotty, hopping in unbridled anticipation.

'Well,' Julian said, 'in a few hours the contents of the tuck shop safe will be ours!'

Night fell over St Gregory's and the spunky chums were all tucked up in bed, pretending to toss in their slumbers. However, at the stroke of midnight Julian put his hands to his lips and made the cry of the school cockerel. The resemblance was uncanny. It sounded just like a restless cock - a sound familiar to everyone in the dorm - but to Tiny and Spotty it was the signal to dress and silently rendezvous by the main staircase.

Silently the chums slipped out and made their way through the school corridors, their pubescent forms silhouetted against the windows by the moonlight that was their only source of illumination.

Moving lithely through the school, their hearts beating like hummingbirds' wings, they quickly reached the tuck shop door. In a move that had been well rehearsed, Julian got down on his knees with Tiny while Spotty kept watch.

Holding a treasured hairclip in his fingers, Julian went to work on the lock, his nimble fingers fiddling as they'd never fiddled before. After what seemed like an eternity Julian's patience was rewarded wih the reassuring 'click'. With perspiration forming on his young brow, Julian gently grasped the large knob and turned it slowly. Pushing in a controlled manner Julian managed to open the door without the tell-tale creaks echoing around the school.

'696969'. In less than a minute Julian had broken the code of the safe and was stuffing florins and ten shilling notes down his and Tiny's underpants.

Suddenly Julian went stiff as a hand grasped him.

'You must hurry!' whispered Spotty. 'I can hear someone coming down the corridor!'

If they hadn't known his schedule they would have sworn that this was Mr Tostovich, the school caretaker on one of his regular night patrols. Whoever was making those determined strides was coming closer and closer.

'It *is* Tossy. I can see his torch!' exclaimed Spotty. 'He's come early!'

'He's heading right this way. If he catches us we'll be in for a jolly good thrashing!' warned Tiny as the steps boomed in the darkness.

Julian's lightning mind considered the consequences.

'It's a tempting proposition alright,' he explained. 'But we've come this far and we've got to go all the way. Spotty, I need your weapon now.'

Spotty withdrew the menacing instrument and handed it to Julian.

'Back against the wall,' ordered their leader. 'He'll be here any moment.'

The footsteps grew louder but, like so many other times before, Julian's agile young body did not fail him. When the shadowy figure turned the corner Julian was ready with his weapon raised. His hand came down deftly. There was a blow, then a muffled cry and a hollow thud as the figure crumpled to the floor. Tiny looked at the darkened form.

'That's not Mr Tostovich!' he said, in a state of shock.

'Crikey,' added Spotty, who had turned the body on to its back. 'It's Matron! Let's scarper!'

'Not so fast chaps!' said Julian, who by now had picked up the fallen torch and was pointing it at the unconscious familiar figure in a blue dress. Bending down he grabbed hold of Matron's curly hair and pulled. The wig came clean off in his hands. 'Look, you fellows. It's not Matron at all. It's Mr Wibbley the Deputy Head!!'

WILL JULIAN BE ABLE TO CONCEAL THE TREASURE HIDDEN IN HIS UNDERPANTS?

WILL THE PLUCKY CHUMS BE ABLE TO WITHDRAW SAFELY?

WHY IS MR WIBBLEY WEARING A BLUE DRESS WHEN RED IS FAR MORE BECOMING?

- Don't miss the next thrilling instalment of
JULIAN PULLS IT OFF

THE REAL MAN AT SCHOOL

My, it seems like only yesterday I was in short trousers. Well, I was, but the public don't need to know that. Things have certainly changed since my days at public school. Then everyone knew their place (usually the Deputy Head's study after lights out) and there was a certain order to things (jacket, tie, trousers, baby lotion...)

I worked my way up, starting as a fag and ending up as a prefect, ruling the First Formers with a rod of iron. Today, instead of prefects it's school bullies who dish out discipline and generally make the younger boys' lives a misery. I was horrified to discover that bullies even have their own fan magazine...

JUNIOR REAL MEN
- HOW TO FORM YOUR OWN REAL BOY GANG OF BULLIES!

RULES OF THE GANG:

★ When choosing a name, why not call yourself after the street you meet on, the school you go to or the estate you all live on? Whatever you do, don't do what I did and name your gang after a gentleman's cologne - or an item of personal delectation, such as that perennial favourite 'The Rich Tea Fingers'.

★ Likewise, if you want a gang symbol to wear on your jackets, choose a dramatic motif, like a death's head, fire-breathing dragon or Harley Davidson rather than a hamster or the Marks & Spencer logo.

★ Prospective members should all have nicknames like Slasher, Bastard, Psycho, Duffer and Hard Man. Anyone called Specky, Gutbucket or Winkle should not only have their membership applications torn up but also their homework books, their stamp collections and their bus passes.

★ Anyone who lost his virginity later than twelve years old can never be considered a full member of the gang.

★ Members should be prepared to wave their genitals around without shame in front of other gang members whenever a joke gets out of hand. (Whilst I was running with a gang called 'The Lancôme Louts', we spent so many afternoons doing precisely this during a ferociously hot summer that it became necessary for Factor 25 to be applied each morning to avoid sunburn.)

★ Gangs should meet in alleyways, in the town precinct, outside Darren's house or in a multi-storey car park. Never schedule meetings for the public lending library, arts centre or aisle three at Tesco's.

★ It is obligatory to fight, scratch or steal cars, smoke, drink, fight, hassle girls from your school and fight. Gangs DO NOT, as a rule, help old people cross the road, tidy up litter, play I-Spy with those silly little books or attempt street theatre. (The Lancôme Louts once caused quite a stir in Swindon when they set themselves up as a mime troupe doing Comedia Del Arte shows in the Arndale Centre for the benefit of tired shoppers).

★ Be ready for well-meaning Channel 4 documentary crews to come along and ask you why you do what you do. They do not want you to say, 'Cos I'm well hard' or 'Cos I'm a young sociopath with a chemical imbalance and a thirty Pritt Sticks a day habit'. What they want you to say is: 'Because of current government policies, there are insufficient leisure facilities in this borough' or 'I'll never be able to get a job so I'm expressing my grievances'.

BULLY4U

60p

★ ALL THE BULLIES! ★ ALL THE ACTION!

★ ALL THE VICTIMISATION!

Bare Knuckle Bonanza Issue!!!

Bodacious!
Start your own protection racket for fun and profit!

Excellent!
28 ways to make a First Year cry!

ACE NEW COMPETITION!!!
Match the bully with his victim and win a pair of 14-hole DMs!!

62 **Party Time!** threatening phrases guaranteed to make victims hand over their lunch money!

Mega!
Psychological torture - will taunting ever replace a good old-fashioned kick to the groin?

Awesome!
Being expelled; why it's not all good!

Well Wicked!
4 new kidney punches to learn and use!

PLUS ALL YOUR REGULAR FEATURES!

■ **ASK ANIMAL:** Our resident Agony Bully writes just for you (with the help of his remedial teacher)

■ **PHOTO FIGHT:** Full length new stories for those who have difficulty reading: "Cry Baby", "First Form Head Butting Frenzy", "Nailed To The Desk", "Term Of Terror", "He's Got My Bag, Sir", "New Boy Funeral Pyre", "No Mercy For Specky" and "Bus Stop Blood Bath"

■ **LIFESTYLE:** Gain 20lbs in ten days!

■ **FASHION:** Designer Bullies - here to stay?

FREE INSIDE!!!
Megadacious Planet-Sized colour poster of St Gregory's heart-throb bully, JOOLS 'THE FIST' CLARY!

SCHOOL

CRIPPLER HOGAN OF 5F WOULD LIKE TO ANNOUNCE THAT HE WILL NO LONGER BE BULLYING 'SMEGGY' HONNOR

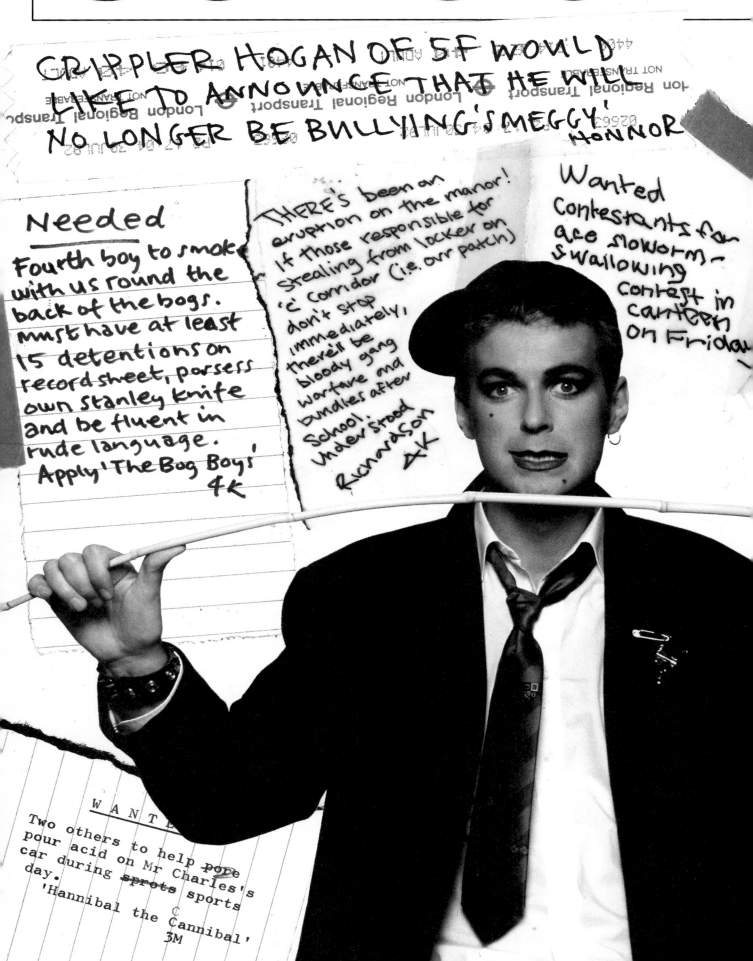

Needed

Fourth boy to smoke with us round the back of the bogs. Must have at least 15 detentions on record sheet, possess own stanley knife and be fluent in rude language. Apply 'The Bog Boys' 4K

THERE'S been an eruption on the manor! If those responsible for stealing from locker on 'C' corridor (i.e. ovr patch) don't stop immediately, there'll be bloody gang warfare and bundles after school. Understood Richardson 4K

Wanted contestants for are slowworm-swallowing contest in canteen on Friday

WANTED
Two others to help pore pour acid on Mr Charles's car during sprots sports day. 'Hannibal the Cannibal' 3M

NOTICES

HEY EVERYONE! I've got monster V.D. and you'd better all not get too near me or even talk to me because it's so virulent and all the slaggy girls in the school had better not go to McDonalds with me anymore. 'Rhino' McCabe. 2p

'Specky' helped me write this advert. He is a really good bloke and I think we should stop emptying his bag into the wheelie bins and all the girls should go out with him, not me.

WANTED

Air Pistol to half-blind a First Year and claim it was an accident.
THUMPER Parrant, 3m.

ENFORCER, wanted for short kid with ideas above his station. Applicants should have previous experience in steaming, rucking, pushing first years down flights of stairs dangling R.E. teachers out of windows and of maiming someone during Tech. Ed. Day = the choice from my tuckbox every lunchtime.
'Shorthouse' 1R.

KAREN GEORGE is a syphy dog 4£ with genital warts(who'll do it with anyone. Wayne. @4H. and it was me that chucked her and not hte other way round..

Wanted

Some weedy kid to bully while 'crybaby' Perkins of 3p is recovering from his last suicide attempt. All applicants to 'turbo' Bates 3m

JUST KIDDING SMEGGY.
SEE YOU AT THE
LAST STOP. YOURS.
CRIPPLER. 5F

A REAL MAN'S BEST FRIEND – HIS REAL DOG

5 REAL DOGS A REAL MAN WOULD NEVER OWN

- ✖ Sausage dog
- ✖ Chihuahua
- ✖ French poodle
- ✖ Any other poodle
- ✖ Any Fanny lookalike

5 REAL DOGS FOR A REAL MAN TO OWN

- ✔ Rottweiler
- ✔ Doberman
- ✔ Pit bull terrier
- ✔ Alsatian
- ✔ Any combination of any of the above

KILLER

I remember those long hot summer days, those romps in the park without a care in the world. People, some of them complete strangers, would come up to me and ask if they could pet my best friend. Well, of course I let them. It gave me such pleasure to hear those familiar sounds of happy panting. But how times have changed. Nowadays there are far too many dangerous dogs around. Real Men flaunt them like sovereign rings or love bites. Call me old-fashioned but it's become far too dangerous to expose my Fanny to any park where a Real Man and his Real Dog might be.

GOOD NAMES FOR YOUR REAL DOG

* Hunter
* Killer
* Ripper
* Shredder
* Mincer (or perhaps not?)
* Crusher
* Destroyer
* Terminator
* Terminator 2
* Mutilator
* Mangler
* Assassin

BAD NAMES FOR YOUR REAL DOG

* Punter
* Toby
* Queenie
* Edward
* Jason
* LuLu
* Floella
* Roger
* Margaret
* Doreen
* Janice
* Ping Pong
* Fanny

GOOD COMMANDS TO TEACH YOUR REAL DOG

- Kill!
- Shred!
- Mince!*
- Crush!
- Destroy!
- Terminate!
- Mutilate
- Sever!
- Maim!
- Disembowel!
- Lacerate!

* as in 'chew', not 'walk'

BAD COMMANDS TO TEACH YOUR REAL DOG

- Sit on my lap!
- Sit on my face!
- Mince!*
- Die for the Queen!
- Bite my trousers!

* as in 'walk', not 'chew'

The Pedigree of the Ideal Real Dog

Good

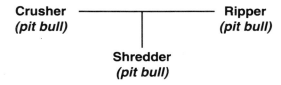

Crusher (pit bull) ——————— Ripper (pit bull)
|
Shredder (pit bull)

Better

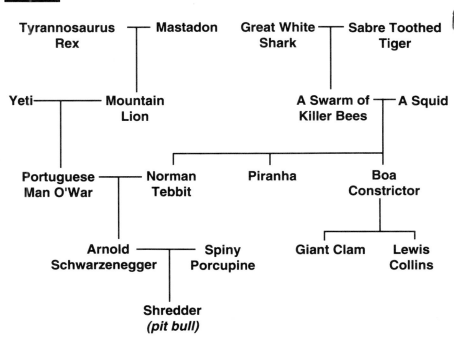

Tyrannosaurus Rex —— Mastadon   Great White Shark —— Sabre Toothed Tiger

Yeti —————— Mountain Lion   A Swarm of Killer Bees —— A Squid

Portuguese Man O'War —— Norman Tebbit   Piranha   Boa Constrictor

Arnold Schwarzenegger —— Spiny Porcupine   Giant Clam   Lewis Collins

Shredder (pit bull)

MY ULTIMATE REAL MAN

No work on Real Men could omit the most masculine man who ever walked God's Fair Earth - the divine Mr Jason Donovan. I'm sure we could all learn so much from him, given the chance. What has he got that other men haven't - and how can we acquire it for our own ends? The joyous Jason unfortunately declined to be interviewed for this book - but I was not deterred, dear reader! Not wanting to admit defeat, I resorted to deception, and elected to probe the lemon-haired pretty boy and part-time Dreamcoat wearer with some penetrating questions in the cunning guise of ordinary fan letters...

JASON DONOVAN

With compliments

Dear Julian,
No, I am not interested in your proposal, but thank you for asking.
Sincerely, Jason Donovan.

JASON DONOVAN

With compliments

Dear Julian,
Yes, cross my heart. Sincerely Ja

JASON DONOVAN

With compliments

Dear Julian,
Yes, I am really sure.
Sincerely, Jason Donovan.

JASON DON

With compliments

Dear Julian,
What a strange question! Sometimes I buy Lurpak, and sometimes I use Flora. I hope that answers your question!
Sincerely, Jason Donovan.

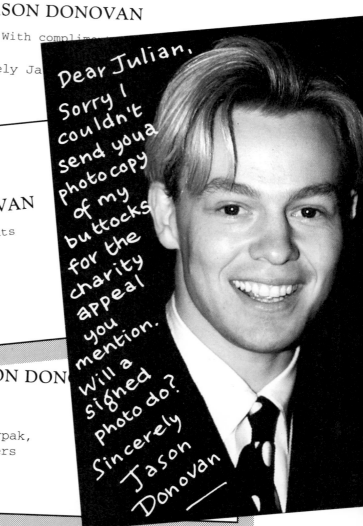

Dear Julian,
Sorry I couldn't send you a photocopy of my buttocks for the charity appeal you mention. Will a signed photo do?
Sincerely
Jason Donovan

JASON DONOVAN

With compliments

Dear Julian,

No, I have never worn a sarong of any description. Why do you ask?
Sincerely, Jason Donovan.

JASON DONOVAN

With compliments

Dear Julian,
Thank you for your letter. The answers to your questions are:
A) No, I have never been a professional wrestler B) No, I don't think
the beige loincloth I wore in 'Joseph' was really me C) Mostly, I
wear pyjamas. D) Yes, my daily exercise routine does include press-
ups and squat thrusts. Sincerely, Jason Donovan

JASON DON

With complim

Dear Julian,
No, I don't want to go to
Eastbourne with you for the weekend.
Sincerely, Jason Donovan.

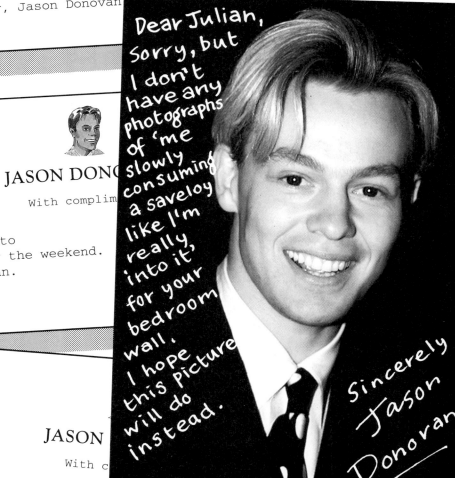

Dear Julian, Sorry, but I don't have any photographs of 'me slowly consuming a saveloy like I'm really into it, for your bedroom wall. I hope this picture will do instead.

Sincerely Jason Donovan

JASON

With c

Dear Julian,
Will you please go away and stop sending me cards and letters and
hanging around outside my house and jumping up at my kitchen window,
waving a fork!
Sincerely, Jason Donovan.

The ADVENTUROUS REAL MAN

Sometimes a man's gotta do what a man's gotta do...

Down the Boozer

Pubs are fun, aren't they? And Real Men's bars are the very best. I mean, who could fail to enjoy a Real Man's watering hole?

For example, where else could you possibly indulge in some 'Old Peculiar'? (Actually, I do know where else, but I'm not divulging - and no, it isn't round Dennis Norden's house.)

When I used to work in the Queen's Arms as a barman and general skivvy, I got to see a lot of the Real Man's drinking rituals close up, and over the next few pages, I'll be bringing you the benefit of that experience.

Actually, I quite enjoyed the work and I think I was good at it too. Asking punters 'What's your pleasure, gents?' just seemed to come naturally to me, as did my work behind the bar. There's no greater pleasure than pulling one with a firm body and a good head and I was more than happy to work for the tips alone. I even enjoyed going around at closing time saying 'Come on, let's be having you...' and 'Come on, sir, get it down you...'

Such happy days.

Now let's move on - I think we're wasting good drinking time...

SOME SIMPLY DARLING DRINKING GAMES

While I admire a man who knows how to handle his liquor*, I am afraid that Real Man demonstrably cannot handle it - so nor should you even try. Instead, try one of these drinking games.

Bottoms up, as they say...

BEETHOVEN
Drink until you can't hear a word anyone is saying.

JOHN MILTON
Drink until you're blind drunk.

HELEN KELLER
Variation on the above.

THE JOHN F. KENNEDY MEMORIAL DRINKING GAME
Eat nothing for two days, then go to the pub and knock back a triple tequila in one go. Bang. Straight to the head.

THE MAGICAL MYSTERY TOUR
Drink double Southern Comforts all night. Wake up somewhere you don't recognise (score bonus points if the people there are speaking either Flemish or Bantu).

DEEP THROAT
A game which sounds far more enjoyable than it really is. Basically, you just drink eighteen pints of snakebite and wake up in casualty with a tube down your throat. The times I've done that...(Ithink)

BLACKOUT
Drink triple Southern Comforts until you find yourself on a bus going somewhere. Have vague recollection of asking the landlord's alsatian if it wants to come to a beach party.

TOM BAKER'S TARDIS DRINKING GAME
Your internal organs will hold approximately fourteen imperial pints of liquid. You must try and alter the laws of time and space by fitting at least 28 pints into them before visiting the little boys' room...

ALTERED STATES
The object is to drink a succession of pints down in one. Every time you fail, you must give your best mate a smacker on the lips. Continue until he starts to look surprisingly good and you start to get a bit liberal with your tongue, by which time he will probably decide the game is well and truly over. (Or perhaps not.)

JUDY GARLAND'S OVER THE RAINBOW DRINKING GAME.
A real favourite down at the Queen's Arms. Drink your way over the rainbow with the following drinks:

Red   - Bloody Mary
Orange   - Vodka and orange juice
Yellow   - Warnincks Advocaat
Green   - Creme de menthe
Blue   - Creme de cacao
Indigo   - Creme de cacao mixed with Martini Rosso
Violet   - Creme de cacao, mixed with Martini Rosso and Guinness

Realise that you're not in Kansas anymore and make your own yellow(ish) brick road all the way home.

*By the ears

WHERE TO FIND A REAL MAN

Maybe you're just curious, maybe you have an ulterior motive; either way, try the following

WATERING HOLES REAL MEN FREQUENT
- Anywhere with a one-word name like Champers, Cheers, Bogart's, or Astaire's
- Anywhere that offers four or more girls a free bottle of bubbly on Thursdays
- Anywhere they still hold 'Miss Wet T-Shirt' contests
- Anywhere where, when they play the *Hawaii 5-0* theme, everybody goes collectively crazy and does silly Polynesian arm movements
- Anywhere that describes itself as 'a fun pub'
- Anywhere the police make a point of driving by regularly

TYPES OF WATERING HOLES TO AVOID
- Anywhere where, when you go up to the bar, they offer you the pub cribbage set and invite you to let your hair down
- Anywhere the average age of the punters is 128
- Anywhere the barman refers to you as 'squire' or 'my good man'
- Anywhere they still hold 'Mr Wet T-Shirt' contests
- Anywhere they know how to vogue properly
- Anywhere with a roaring fire and an inglenook
- Anywhere where the punters are eating cold salmon and drinking Britvics
- Anywhere that zebra and wildebeeste congregate to drink at twilight

PUB SNACKS

I think that pub snacks are truly revolting, but Real Men consume them avidly, so I suppose you should too. It's just that I can't bring myself to indulge with you, that's all.

Dry roasted nuts sound just so unappealing, while in my experience there is nothing on earth more off-putting than a Cheesy Ringo being thrust in front of you. Even watching men filling their mouths with Wotsits is not the thrill it could be.

I have been known to put the odd pork scratching in my mouth (while on holiday in Morocco), but I really couldn't say if I swallowed it or not.

While serving in the Queen's Arms, I had the opportunity to study many hundreds of bodies and to learn all the secrets of body language that Real Men show when they're out for a good time.

To compensate for his lack of eloquence, the Real Man has developed a complex body language to help him say exactly what he means... ▶

Dancing to attract the opposite sex is an activity as old as man himself.

Since the purpose is to attract a mate, rather than stimulate the one you have, Real Men often do little dances together at the bar to attract female attention, to show what fun individuals they are and to display their raw unbridled sexuality. It is at no time meant to indicate a homosexual disposition. ▼

BODY LANGUAGE AT THE BAR

Touch my pint and I'll have you!

You're...my...best mate in the whole world!

RITUAL MALE DANCING

The can-can, not particularly easy to do to 'Sweet Child of Mine', but still manageable...

Likewise, hand jiving to Kenny Rogers' 'The Gambler' is tricky, but rewarding.

TIME GENTLEMEN PLEASE...

I really would like to be served now, thank you!

I'm not really on the pull but...

Bryan Adams music is not, strictly speaking, conga music. However, persevere - and you never know who might wrap their arms around you!

Now you have the girls' attention, really start to pile it on with some virtuoso dancing...

CONTINUED OVER...

...ending in a spectacular finish!

Good, someone's put 'Tears of a Clown' on the jukebox. Time for a singalong to show that you're good lads as well as sexy as all hell.

Then one of your friends suddenly decides to show his age and spoils everything...

...resulting in a thorough slapping with a rolled-up cocktail menu and another evening spent alone and frustrated in the boudoir.

TAUNTING THE POLICE

The art of taunting and baiting police officers does largely depend upon the sort of policeman you come across...

BAD THINGS TO SAY TO THE POLICE	
• You'll never take me alive, copper	• Here's 10p. Forget you ever saw me, OK?
• I'm armed!	• It's in my left hand pocket...
• Kick me in the balls – I won't press charges!	• Let him have it, Chris!

How to have credibility down the Working Man's Club...

The Working Man's Club is the Real Man's version of a club in St James. Here, if your face fits, you'll always find a welcome amongst like-minded individuals. But, just like with those exclusive men's clubs, you first have to prove that you're really 'one of them'... How hard can that be?

FANNY'S PIN-UP PET OF THE MONTH

Wouldn't you like to be in season when Butch here is sniffing around the neighbourhood? Certainly not the runt of the litter, Butch is a Real Dog who could tempt any lapdog to stray, with his muscular frame and movie star looks (he's already appeared in a number of highly successful dogfighting videos!). Isn't it a pity he's had to have his 'packed lunch' removed by law?

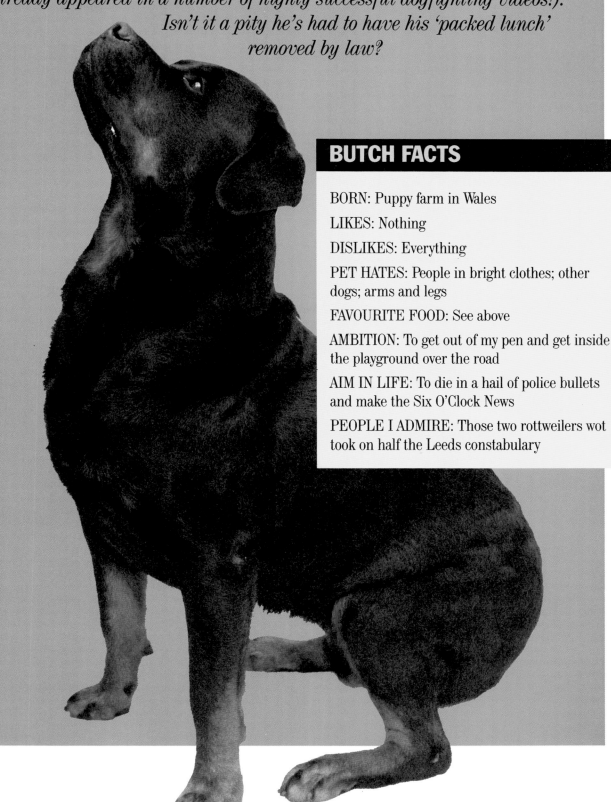

BUTCH FACTS

BORN: Puppy farm in Wales

LIKES: Nothing

DISLIKES: Everything

PET HATES: People in bright clothes; other dogs; arms and legs

FAVOURITE FOOD: See above

AMBITION: To get out of my pen and get inside the playground over the road

AIM IN LIFE: To die in a hail of police bullets and make the Six O'Clock News

PEOPLE I ADMIRE: Those two rottweilers wot took on half the Leeds constabulary

MONEY TALKS

I don't like using cash - it's bad taste to reveal your wad in the middle of a crowded store. I much prefer credit cards. They're very flexible and that's an important consideration for someone like me. Most Real Men prefer cash. I don't know why, I've never had anyone refuse me Access.

Cash is so important to them, they've even developed their own special language for it. Now you know me, readers. Always willing to get my tongue around new diction. You can often find me on a wet afternoon in the library, attempting to come to grips with sticky bits of the vernacular. Well, recently I picked up something very interesting. You've probably heard of a 'Monkey' meaning £500 and a 'Pony' meaning £25. Well, there's a few more of these terms, which I never knew existed...

Brontosaurus	£1,000,000
Gorilla	£1,000
Funnel Web Spider	£757.54
Orang Utan	£750
Monkey	£500
Flying Squirrel	£191.50
Pony	£25
Amoeba	£0.01

REAL MEN DON'T...
LIE BACK AND THINK OF ENGLAND
(EXCEPT WHEN THERE'S A MATCH ON)

Great Images of Masculinity

THE
Wild
ONE

BUILDER

Isn't construction fascinating? Whenever I walk past a building site I always stop and have a jolly good look at all the erections in progress. It's amazing how fast some of them go up. One minute they're not there and the next - 'Whoosh' - there's this gleaming whopper staring you in the face, casting a shadow from one side of the street to the other.

In fact, I was standing at just such a construction site the other day, watching the men going about their business, when the site foreman came over to me and said, 'Take your pick and get to work.'

'Well,' I said, 'I'm quite spoiled for choice...'

Before I knew it I was one of them. I helped this particularly charming chap called Dave by filling his hod and relieving him of his load whenever the need arose. And he was very grateful, let me tell you.

WHAT TO WEAR

On a building site you're outside in all weathers and it's so easy to catch a chill. That's why choosing the right clothing when the temperature drops is so important. Here's a handy cut-out-and-keep reference table for the cold weather:

TEMPERATURE	WHAT TO WEAR
10°C	T-shirt and jeans
5°C	T-shirt and jeans
0°C (Freezing)	T-shirt and jeans
-5°C	T-shirt and jeans
-10°C	T-shirt and jeans
-15°C	T-shirt and jeans
-20°C	Sweatshirt and jeans
-25°C	Sweatshirt, jeans and muff
	(Not really, I just like the word!)

JULIAN GOES TO HOLLYWOOD

T here are some things which eternally puzzle and torment Real Men - like why the pubs don't stay open until six in the morning, why can't XR3i's go at 400 mph - and who is the hardest of the hard men? God knows, I've been looking for the answer to that one myself for many years.

Every Real Man has his own opinion. Is Arnie harder than Sly Stallone? Could Chuck Norris take Jean-Claude Van Damme?

A while ago, I asked myself exactly those same questions - and a brilliant idea suddenly hit me: why not write a screenplay for a film starring

ALL of Hollywood's hard men? What a sensation it would be! And, while I was at it, why not write myself a part in the film, so that I could find out what these macho superstars were really made of, and use it to help me research this book!

Inspired, I immediately sat down at the type-writer with just these few idle thoughts in my head and a giant-sized Mars Bar for succour. I laboured on deep into the night, my fingers a blur, my mouth covered in sticky brown stuff. By sunrise, I had completed the screenplay for what I was sure would prove to be one of the most semi-nal films in the history of Hollywood - Hard Men.

Obviously, there's not room to reprint all 397 pages of my man-uscript in this book, but here's an early scene which is fairly representa-tive of Hard Men as a whole... I hope you like it.

(I LOOK UP AND SEE SYLVESTER STALLONE)

JULIAN: Sly! Is that a recoil-less rocket launcher you're holding - or are you just pleased to see me?

STALLONE: I'm just pleased to see you.

JULIAN: How sweet! Why are you standing on a very big box?

STALLONE: Hey, you said you wuzn't gonna mention dat! I may be lacking in inches...

JULIAN: That's not what I heard. Do your worst, Sly!

(SYLVESTER STALLONE WRESTLES ME TO THE GROUND, BUT HE CANNOT KEEP A GRIP ON ME AS THE PEANUT BUTTER TANKER, WHICH CRASHED IN THE PREVIOUS SCENE, HAS SPILLED ITS LOAD ALL OVER THE FLOOR. SYLVESTER AND I SLIP AND SLIDE AROUND, TRYING TO GET A GRIP ON EACH OTHER FOR WHAT MUST SEEM LIKE AGES. FINALLY...)

STALLONE: Gotcha!

JULIAN: (MUFFLED) Sly! Sly! Must you grip me so roughly?

STALLONE: Tell me the secret of thermonuclear particle acceleration and dissolution theory!

JULIAN: (MUFFLED) You're in for a long wait...

(FIFTEEN MINUTES PASS, AND NOTHING MUCH HAPPENS - UNTIL ARNOLD SCHWARZENEGGER APPEARS)

SCHWARZENEGGER: Hey... let... me... deal... mit... this, Sylvester!

(ARNOLD SCHWARZENEGGER GRABS ME)

JULIAN: Arnie! Tee-hee-hee! How did you know I was - hee hee - get off - so ticklish!

(THIS GOES ON FOR QUITE SOME TIME, UNTIL DOLPH LUNDGREN ENTERS)

LUNDGREN: That ain't gonna work, Arnie. But (PRODUCES A COMFY-LOOKING FLUFFY SLIPPER) a sound slippering just might help loosen his tongue...

(THE SLIPPERING WHICH FOLLOWS, WHILE BRIEF, **MUST LOOK ABSOLUTELY AUTHENTIC**. TO ACHIEVE THIS, SOMETHING IN THE REGION OF THIRTY TAKES MAY BE REQUIRED)

JULIAN: Well, that was bracing. Thank you, gentlemen.

LUNDGREN: Jeez, this British guy is tough. I once had Steven Segal begging for mercy after four slaps on the back of his legs with a gym plimsoll! Hey, here comes Chuck Norris! Maybe he'll know how to break this guy.

(ENTER CHUCK NORRIS)

NORRIS: I see you caught Clary - but he ain't talking, huh? You guys tried taking off all your clothes, then putting on high-heel stiletto shoes and walking up and down on his back, singing classic Edith Piaf numbers?

SCHWARZENEGGER: (SLAPPING HIS FOREHEAD) Damn...it...was...so...obvious... too...

(SCHWARZENEGGER, NORRIS, STALLONE AND LUNDGREN PROCEED TO STRIP OFF AND THEN PUT ON SOME RATHER STYLISH BUT WICKEDLY POINTED STILETTO SHOES AND TAKE IT IN TURNS TO WALK UP AND DOWN MY BACK, SINGING 'JE NE REGRETTE RIEN'...THIS IS A POWERFUL MOMENT IN THE FILM AND THE AUDIENCE MUST BE ALLOWED TO SAVOUR IT, EVEN IF IT ADDS ANOTHER THIRTY MINUTES TO THE FILM'S RUNNING TIME, WHICH IT PROBABLY WILL IF I HAVE MY WAY)

JULIAN: I'll tell you nothing!

NORRIS: I just don't believe it! It worked on Nick Nolte!

SCHWARZENEGGER: Huhhh! The... effort... has... made... my... body... glisten... with... lots...of...sweat...

(VOICE FROM OFF): Stand aside, gentlemen. There's only one kind of language that Mr Clary understands...

JULIAN: (SURPRISED) Sean Connery! What are you doing here? And why are you wearing that frogman's outfit?

The lovely Russell has also been screen tested recently for the John Travolta role in a remake of *Saturday Night Fever*. It's provisionally entitled *My Two Left Feet*

Then, in a fit of excitement, my magnum opus clasped firmly in one hand and knife and fork in the other, I jumped aboard the first airliner for Hollywood, ready to 'do lunch' with some of the most powerful men in the business!

Quel dommage! How soon my dreams were shattered! Almost everybody in Hollywood was 'tied up in a meeting' that day. And the few producers who would speak to me didn't want to do lunch. (What they wanted to do we shan't go into here.)

Miffed and peeved, I decided to approach the actors themselves and, although no deals were struck, I was (several times). So no joy there (except when Sean Penn himself slapped me around the thighs with a rolled up copy of Variety).

I decided that, if I was not to become a big name Hollywood scriptwriter like...like...er...well, like a big name Hollywood scriptwriter, perhaps I was approaching this from the wrong direction. (That's the story of my life, I'm afraid.) I simply couldn't believe there wasn't a place for me in Tinseltown, so perhaps I should attempt to become a movie star instead.

Well, to cut a long story short, I soon discovered that, while the casting couch may be dead, the casting top of a desk, the casting jacuzzi, the casting water bed, the casting dungeon fantasy room, the casting rug in front of the fireplace, the casting cabin up in the hills, the casting Best Western motel and the casting in bed with five senior film executives and a marsupial of indeterminate gender are all still very much alive, thank you. It was so humiliating! I knew I had that certain something and so did they - and they were all too eager to get their hands on it as well.

Well, punters, I wasn't about to stoop to that. I knew I had it in me to succeed - without having it in me to succeed, if you catch my drift.

Thank goodness, my luck finally changed and I met some decent producers, who showed genuine interest in my talents, offered me auditions and asked who was handling me. I said no one at the moment, but if I met the right person, that could all change.

Well, I think it's fair to say that I had a fair crack of the whip as a movie star, but Dame Fortune once again decided to turn away her smiling face and every project I worked on seemed to fall through for one reason or another...

FILMS I CAN'T DECIDE WHETHER I'D WANT TO BE IN OR NOT

* LITTLE BIG MAN

FILMS I COULDN'T BE IN

* SHE'S HAVING A BABY

FILMS I COULDN'T BE IN (BUT WISH I COULD)

* STEAMBOAT WILLIE
(Sounds like enormous fun, but unfortunately it's a cartoon)

When *Clary met Sally* was doomed from the start, I suppose. We quickly realised that audiences wouldn't expect much in the way of plot development - and they would have been right too.

A still from my screen test for the title role in *JFK*. (I am told I bear an uncanny resemblance to the young President Kennedy, but since I never attended any of those 'secret White House parties' in the early sixties, I can't comment on that.)

I'M SORRY. NOT ON A FIRST DATE

My screen test for *ALIEN 3*

My screen test for *Basic Instinct*. Michael Douglas's mum burst into tears and I lost the role...

Intended as a starring vehicle for yours truly, I was all set to do this remake of the classic Stephen King creepy - when the studio suddenly realised that it was stupid to go through all this effort just for the sake of a bad pun and cancelled the project.

EXPOSED

THE REAL MAN'S WALLET

I'm always intrigued by the big bulge in a Real Man's pocket. Well, I was willing to risk it for a biscuit (or just a few crumbs if the truth be known). So the other day I went up to one of them and asked to see what he was carrying. Well, he thrust his hand in and pulled out his wallet. I was disappointed. With all that nonsense inside it I can't see why he didn't use a smart, practical clutch bag like mine. Some people have no sense of style.

★ The wallet in all its glory; fake Fake Gucci. Bought in a Torremolinos market for £4.20

★ 2 condoms bought in 1990 in a moment of bravado. (There were originally three but one was used instead of gum at an acid house party in 1991 when someone gave him half an 'E' and he needed something to chew on)

★ Ford Transit Owners Club membership card

★ Club 18-30 reunion reminder

★ Library ticket (used only once when he desperately needed a Haynes manual for his mate's Capri 2.8i)

★ Name and telephone number of someone he met in a pub who got him fake Lacoste polo shirts, two for under £5. (They shrink in under one wash. He's had some for six months now, but hasn't found this out)

★ 18 Embassy gift vouchers. (Only 1,972 more needed for that electric screwdriver)

★ Receipt for a pair of lime green, day-glo polyester and cotton bermuda shorts. (£4.99 at Mr Byrite. Très chic)

★ Piece of paper with a girl's phone number on it. (He met her at a bar last week but has neither the nerve nor the inclination to phone her up. It doesn't really matter since it's a false number anyway - she only wrote something down so he would stop pestering her)

★ Top Man Platinum Charge Card. (It says more about you than money ever can)

★ Video club membership card, dog-eared from overuse

CLARY RAYNER
THE REAL MAN'S AGONY AUNT

Now I like to think of myself as being caring, you know, willing to bend over backwards to help someone, which is why a lot of my friends come to me with their problems. Take the lovely Russell, for instance. He told me he wanted to get a load off his chest. 'Well,' I said. 'Have you tried damp Kleenex? It always works for me.' Now, whenever Real Men ask me for advice I try to be frank and forthright. Trouble is, I really don't understand what's bothering them.

Dear Julian,
I've been going out with my new girlfriend for about 40 minutes now. I keep asking her to go to bed with me but she says she wants to wait until she knows me better. What should I do?
D.K.,Hendon

Dear D.K.
I've never been in this situation, but I think perhaps the moment has passed. Better luck next time.

Dear Julian,
I have a fourteen-inch penis. Is this unusual?
R.S., Fulham

Dear R.S.
I have already replied to you under separate cover (hope Tuesday at 7.00 is convenient).

Dear Julian,
I make love to my wife at about 11.45 every Saturday night after the big film. She says this takes the spontaneity out of our sex life and wants me to change this routine. Can you recommend a more exciting love life?
T.P., Glasgow

Dear T.P.
I always find that Jim'll Fix It *does it for me.*

Dear Julian,
After I've been drinking 12 or 13 pints of an evening and go home I can't seem to get it up. This is annoying my girlfriend who says I should cut back on my drinking so our love life can improve. I've got to choose between my girl and my booze. What should I do?
S.T., Bristol

Dear S.T.
I agree with your girlfriend. Cut down on the pints. I've always found Babycham *a refreshing beverage and, if truth be known, a bit of an aphrodisiac.*

Dear Julian,
A mate of mine says that it's really good fun going to bed with two birds at the same time. I mentioned this to my girlfriend who just slapped me round the face and hasn't spoken to me since. Was I wrong?
F.D., Leeds

Dear F.D.
Why are you asking me?

Dear Julian,
My wife is bored with the way we make love. She wants to try new and exciting things. Can you recommend anything really wonderful?
P.K., Swindon

Dear P.K.
Yes, but first you'll have to divorce her, then buy some lemon curd and a bicycle pump. Good luck.

HOW TO WALK LIKE A REAL MAN

The right way

The wrong way
(but still rather
entrancing and
captivating for
all that)

The completely stupid way

Things a Real Man will never admit to-

★ Failing to get the top off the HP bottle
★ Not fancying Kylie Minogue
★ Knowing where the clitoris is
★ Or caring
★ Crying during *Who Will Love My Children?*
★ That night in Portsmouth docks

FUN OUTINGS WITH THE LADS

THE SEASIDE   Everybody pile into your mate's Cavalier and go to the seaside. Wander up and down the front. Say, 'Alright gels?' to 25-50 different women without any response. Have a go on 'Afterburner' at the arcade. See if there's anyone topless on the beach (there isn't). Drink a few pints. Eat a carton of chips from the pier. Feel sick. Be sick. Say, 'Well, that was crap'. Go home again. (NB Don't hang around under the pier at dusk unless you want to meet homosexuals.)

HOW TO BE A REAL MAN IN BED

This lies a little outside of my province but, as I understand it, it is a time-honoured tradition amongst Real Men that the woman should get no pleasure from making love. Now, as women become ever more liberated and learn advanced lovemaking techniques from the pages of Cosmopolitan, *it's becoming increasingly difficult to ensure that they get nothing at all out of the act - and quite staggering lengths of incompetence and insensitivity are called for.*

However, Real Men still seem to be managing it somehow.

So, if you want to be a Real Man in bed, here's some ways in which you can ruin your partner's pleasure (I think).

FOREPLAY

She's had ten minutes of Mick Hucknall and half a glass of Lambrusco; you've told her you think she's 'a really tasty bird' (I think that's Russell's latest gambit...) - what more does she need to get her going?

Time to move on...

POST-COITAL CRUELTY

Simply say something like:

* You made it, you sleep in it!
* I needed that! I was so desperate I would have shagged anything.
* I hope you go home before I sober up

HOW TO MAKE YOURSELF CLIMAX FASTER

I am certain that Real Men do it from start to finish in under 90 seconds because they are deliberately trying to prevent the woman from getting any pleasure.

If you can't usually manage this yourself, try thinking of:

* Selina Scott in the remake of *Flashdance*
* Two topless girls driving along in an XR3i cabriolet
* Princess Di in a black leather catsuit cracking a huge bull's pizzle whip and snarling 'Suck my four-inch stiletto heels or I'll flay your worthless bottom until it's red-raw, you spineless wretch!' (This might take some imagination)

INTERCOURSE

1) Keep ruining the mood by throwing in the odd (or indeed very odd) whispered sweet nothing, like:
* You know what I keep wondering about? What's under Shane Richie's foreskin?
* Go on: you did, you did. You let one off, didn't you?
* Do you think Ronald McDonald's got a penis?
* You ain't nearly as good as your sister...
* Oy! Is the dog in bed with us or have you forgotten to shave your legs again?

2) Make liberal use of your elbows. Stick them in all the most uncomfortable and unwelcome places you can think of. (L L Cool J once poked me with his elbow but this isn't something I'd expect the average mortal to manage.)

NOTE: Whatever you do, don't let her get on top. She'll think you're a 'New Man' for sure and start pestering you to borrow all your Sting albums...

HOW TO GIVE A GIRL 'THE LOOK'

Improving your love life

It doesn't matter how full or how lacking a Real Man's sex life actually is - as long as all your friends think you're getting more than your fair share.

You know that nothing happened again on Saturday night; no one wanted to know you in the pub so you went home and finally fell asleep in front of *The Thirty Nine Steps* with your mouth half full of semi-masticated special fried noodles. But your mates don't.

That's why you must tell them that you had the most extraordinary sexual adventures instead. Feel no shame, dear reader. After all, they're lying to you as well.

A GOOD BOAST
YOU: You'll never guess who I shagged Saturday! Only Princess Stephanie of Monaco!
YOUR MATE: You don't half pull some great birds, Tony!
A BAD BOAST
YOU: I had Princess Margaret Saturday night
YOUR MATE: Any good?

GOOD PEOPLE TO BOAST THAT YOU HAD LAST SATURDAY NIGHT
✔ Gloria Hunniford
✔ Last Tuesday's Starbird
✔ Sharon Stone
✔ Caron Keating
✔ Michaela Strachan
✔ Judith Chalmers
✔ All the Nolan Sisters
✔ Cheryl Baker

GOOD THINGS TO CLAIM YOUR PARTNER SAID
✔ Yes
✔ It's so long - I can hardly see the end of it
✔ You're better than your mate
✔ I'll call the *Guinness Book of Records* tomorrow
✔ You've spoiled me for every other man now
✔ You're the best I've ever had - or my name isn't Dannii Minogue!
✔ Didn't I see you on stage with the Chippendales?
✔ God! You've lasted longer than the British monarchy!

BAD PEOPLE TO BOAST THAT YOU HAD LAST SATURDAY NIGHT
✘ Danny Baker
✘ Any female MP
✘ The person you're talking to's wife
✘ The person you're talking to's daughter
✘ That woman with all the carrier bags who wanders around the town centre, spitting at the pigeons
✘ The 'wolf girl' of Uruguay, as featured in last week's *Sunday Sport*
✘ The Queen Mum
✘ Prince Edward
✘ Yourself

BAD THINGS TO CLAIM YOUR PARTNER SAID
✘ No
✘ Ta-da! I'm really a man called Brian! Surprise!!!
✘ Never mind, dear, it's what you do with it that counts
✘ I was expecting a one night stand, not a one minute stand
✘ Oh, they've reintroduced rationing, have they?
✘ Now that's what I call a truly sad one!
✘ Wait until I tell all the other members of Def Leppard

GIRLIE MAGS

Just the other day I was in my local sweet shop. I had one of my recurring sore throats and was looking for a Fisherman's Friend to suck when my eye suddenly wandered up to the top shelf of the magazine racks. Why this should happen, I just don't know. Call it uncanny and unnatural if you like. One minute I was looking for something to pop in my mouth and the next, well, I was looking at a girlie mag.

I was shocked. I couldn't believe what I was seeing or reading. It was disgusting and I don't know how publishers have the nerve!

Now if I was editor of a girlie mag I'd print features that I know readers would find stimulating...

Marvellous Entertainment for Real Men

Real MEN ONLY

Not for sale to anyone under 5' (they won't be able to reach it on the top shelf)

NOV 1992 £2.00

ATTENTION Mr Newsagent: Don't you wish you didn't have to get up at such an ungodly hour just so you could sort out the newspaper deliveries. I really like a lie in so I'm glad I don't have your job.

SOME LIKE IT HOT!
Cheryl, our cookery expert, looks at traditional Mexican cuisine

IN BED WITH TINA!
Bold floral prints dominate this stylish boudoir

LICK YOUR LIPS WITH ERICA!
Wouldn't you like to get your hands on her mouth-watering recipe for apple flan?

BLONDES HAVE MORE FUN!
Hair colouring made simple

SULTRY SAMANTHA'S BIG TIPS!
Comprehensive hints and advice on make-up, skin care and dieting

DOGGIE FASHION!
Pamper your pet with these stylish little raincoats

LYNN THE EXHIBITIONIST!
This beautiful red head shows how to display dried flowers for maximum effect

KAREN BARES ALL!
This Page 3 stunner reveals her taste in costume jewellery!

HAPPY HOOKERS!
Crochet for Beginners

A question of size

Are there really some men out there who are hung like draught excluders? I for one usually find that hard to swallow.

However, the Real Man is, and always will be, obsessed with the size of his best friend, however much he may deny it. He's also obsessed with the size of his best friend's 'best friend' too.

I don't believe that any of the gadgets currently on sale can help you if you feel that you can never be a Real Man because of some little deficiency down there, but for the sake of thoroughness in this book (and out of a prurient sense of curiosity which I will deny henceforth) I went in search of larger than average men. After all, if there really were 'big men' out there, I wanted to know; I wanted to be clued up and filled in.

What happened? Well, I came away empty is all I can say.

However, I then embarked on a series of...rather unorthodox... experiments to see if there was any way in which I could help you to become 'real big men'...

REAL MEN DON'T...
USE CUCUMBERS

Test No 1:

The domestic vacuum cleaner with hose attachment

Subject's comments: "Everybody in casualty was very sympathetic. They said they were quite used to treating people with their appendages firmly wedged in domestic appliances, because, apparently, people often vacuum the house in the nude and have accidents, especially on Friday and Saturday nights."

Results: The organ's measured size was actually found to be smaller than before, even after the skin grafts.

Test No 2:

Exposure to radioactive elements (there is some evidence that radioactivity can cause giant mutations)

Subject's comments: "What's the point in having a bigger one when all your teeth are falling out and your ears light up in the dark?"

Results: The test organ has indeed grown. However, it is also fluorescent green and lows like a calf. Good fun at acid house parties but otherwise a social hindrance.

Test No 3:

The Wasp Box (A large wooden box into which first the penis and then a swarm of enraged wasps is placed. The box is secured firmly around the waist by means of a belt)

Subject's comments: "Please, no...I...I can feel them buzzing all round me...take it off now...ahhh! PLEASE! OUCH!...NO! NO!...AHHHHHHHH! AHHH! OWWWWWWWWWWWWWWWWW!

Results: Some temporary swelling which, although promising, was accompanied by a total loss of sex drive.

Test No 4:

MAGIC, as performed on the naked subject by the great Renaldo and his lovely assistant Stephanie.

Subject's comments: "I felt a right wally. Why did it have to be the Palladium on a Saturday night?"

Results: No improvement, but subject now ejaculates bunches of flowers and knotted handkerchiefs.

HOW TO CHUCK YOUR GIRLFRIEND

WRONG WAY

I'M SORRY TRACY BUT IT'S NO GOOD. YOU SEE I'M AN ARIES AND, WELL, YOU'RE A SCORPIO AND WE'RE NOT REALLY COMPATIBLE. YOU WANT TO SETTLE DOWN AND START A FAMILY WHILE I WANT TO MAKE A CAREER OUT OF ACCOUNTING. THE SKY'S THE LIMIT WHEN YOU'VE GOT QUALIFICATIONS IN DOUBLE ENTRY BOOK KEEPING AND I'M DETERMINED TO REACH THE TOP NO MATTER WHAT IT TAKES. I'M SORRY IT DIDN'T WORK OUT, I TRULY AM, BUT I LOVE YOU EVER SO DEARLY. THERE'LL ALWAYS BE A PLACE IN MY HEART FOR YOU AND BLAH, BLAH, BLAH...

TRACY... THE WEDDING'S OFF TOMORROW. BYE!

RIGHT WAY

FUN OUTINGS WITH THE LADS

THE VIDEO SHOP ★ Snatch up a porno film, take it up to the girl behind the counter and ask, "Are you in this one, luv?"

★ Starting arguing who's the best - Jean-Claude Van Damme or Chuck Norris - and then decide to settle it by having a mock kick fight around the Family Drama racks.

★ Persuade the person serving you to tell you the address of the unfortunate punter who's hired *An Evening With Les Dennis* then go round to their house and wake them up.

What you wear says so much about you, wouldn't you agree? At first glance, the Real Man appears to put no thought into his apparel, but look closer. He generally avoids chiffon (a wise choice with stubble), fluorescent pink lycra body stockings and anything else that might get him in trouble up the Kilburn High Road. So he does think about what he wears after all. Quelle surprise!

This is wise. After all, even the most Real of Real Men start to lose their masculine appeal when they deviate from the straight and true. Take Mel Gibson (chance would be a fine thing). He is the yardstick. Even the mean, moody and magnificent Mel can look completely different in the wrong sort of clothing.

Try it for yourself.

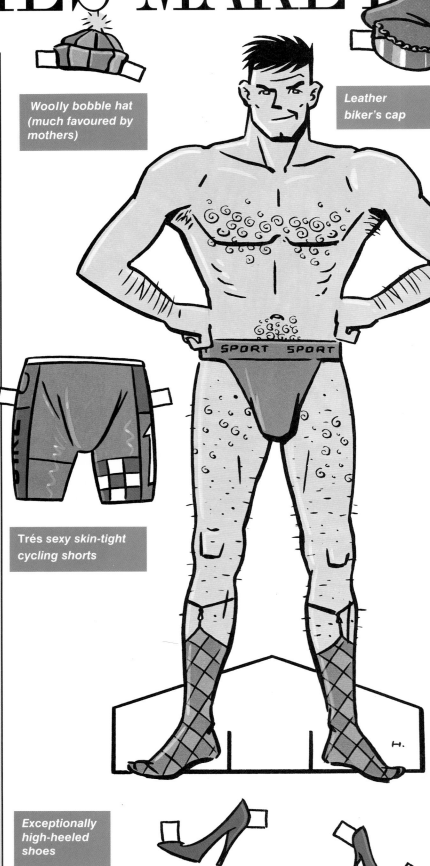

Woolly bobble hat (much favoured by mothers)

Leather biker's cap

Trés sexy *skin-tight* cycling shorts

Exceptionally high-heeled shoes

THE (REAL) MAN

Real Man at C&A bomber jacket

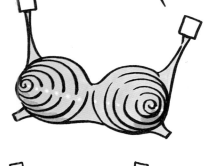

Bring-the-house-down Madonna bra

Nipple peek-a-boo T-shirt

Leopardskin leotard

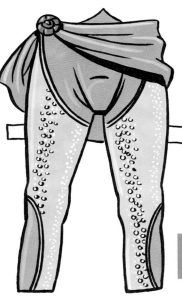

My favourite outfit

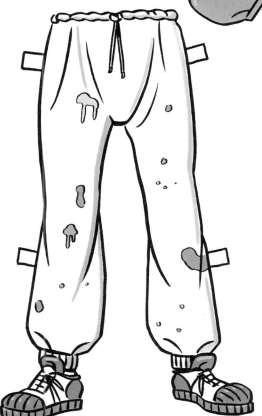

Baggy, paint-spattered track suit bottoms and trainers

ALSO AVAILABLE FOR YOUR MEL GIBSON DOLLY

- The pride of Laura Ashley
- Feather boa
- M & S slip
- Silk Janet Reger nightie
- Pervy gymslip
- Darryl Hannah blonde wig
- 'Emma Peel' leather cat suit
- Naughty 'Spartacus' dressing up set
- Darling Judy's outfit from The Wizard of Oz
- Stockings, suspenders and a garter belt
- T-shirt with Jason Donovan on it

Great Images of Masculinity

REBEL WITHOUT ANY DRESS SENSE

HAVING AN AFFAIR

All Real Men have affairs. It's accepted - but most at least try to hide it from their partners and can come up with excuses when challenged by their wives. She wants to hear that you love her, that she's the only one for you, that you still care...

THE WRONG THINGS TO SAY WHEN YOUR WIFE ACCUSES YOU OF HAVING AN AFFAIR WITH ANOTHER WOMAN

★ Yes I am
★ What's it to you?
★ Yes I am, but it's with your sister, so it doesn't really count
★ Yes I am, but it's with my sister, so it doesn't really count
★ Of course I'm not. I'm homosexual
★ Who wants to know?
★ Quoi? Je ne comprends pas l'anglais. Je suis français
★ Everything I do is wrong to you, isn't it?
★ I was driven into her arms by your smell

THE STAG NIGHT

Isn't it funny that although there's absolutely no chance of me ever getting married (well, unless the rumours are true about that trendy vicar in Reading) some of the marriage terms bring on a feeling of déjà vu. *Like 'tying the knot' or 'getting hitched' - and as for 'getting spliced' or 'exchanging rings', well, the public don't need to know about that. I've already resigned myself to missing out on a 'Stag*

Night'. Quel dommage. *But for a Real Man, the next Stag Night is the highlight of his social calendar (well, that and the drinking sprees every Saturday night). Apart from the chance to get even more legless than usual, the Stag Night is often your last chance to talk your friends out of getting married and try to get them to have strange sex with the now obligatory kiss-o-gram.*

A cut-out and keep guide

GOOD & BAD PLACES FOR A STAG NIGHT

Good
- Amsterdam
- Hamburg
- A schoolgirls' dormitory
- Princess Di's bedroom
- A massage parlour
- In a jacuzzi with two Penthouse Pets

Bad
- John O'Groats
- Swindon
- An old people's home
- Prince Edward's bedroom
- Below decks on HMS *Invincible*
- The rhino enclosure at London Zoo

KISS-O-GRAMS
Good Grams
- Re-enactment Of *9½ Weeks*-o-Gram
- Identical Twins With Their Own Tubs Of Flora-o-Gram
- Sixth Form Girls With Gymslips Two Sizes Too Small-o-Gram
- Young Swedish Au Pair With No Clothes And No Inhibitions-o-Gram
- Hot 'n' Ready For It And Won't Say No-o-Gram

Bad Grams
- Don't Realise It's A Transvestite Until It's Too Late-o-Gram
- Septic Bag Lady-o-Gram
- Blow-Up Doll With Face Like Nana Mouskouri-o-Gram
- Grit Under The Foreskin-o-Gram
- Crunchy Peanut Butter Enema-o-Gram

IMPORTANT! THE ONE PLACE WHERE THE GROOM *HAS* TO END UP

- Naked, bound, gagged and chained to a lamppost with biscuits up his behind

RUMOURS SPREAD BY REAL MEN TO PREVENT THEIR MATES FROM GETTING MARRIED

- You'll suddenly suffer from premature ejaculation
- You'll have to stay in Friday nights and watch *Brookside* and *Casualty* with your wife instead of going on a great drinking binge with your mates
- Your wife will murder you for the insurance money
- Your in-laws will murder you because they're in league with your wife
- You'll only have sex on your birthday
- You'll have to buy a house and then the mortgage rate will go up to 38 per cent and you won't be able to pay it and your house'll be repossessed and you'll have to move in with your in-laws.Forever.
- All your money will be wasted on curtains and bedspreads and rubbish like that
- You'll find she's got an old flatulent granny who'll have to move in with you and make you feel sick at mealtimes

Performing in a male dance troupe

Muscular, glistening, firm male bodies, pulsating to hot rock music, snake-like hips gyrating sinu-ously, prominent male organs barely contained in sequined G-strings strained almost to breaking point...
I suppose it must appeal to somebody.

Male dance troupes, like The Chippendales and The Dream Boys, seem to be all the rage these days. Now, I know a good thing when I see one (it comes with experience), which is why I have now formed my very own dance troupe - Julian's Joy Boys.

JULIAN CLARY

Presents

JULIAN'S JOY BOYS

90 minutes of solid (and we do mean solid) male bodies, erotic dancing, sensuous stripping and G-strings pinging off in your face just when you're trying to enjoy your choc ice on a stick

COME ONE - COME ALL!

I personally try out all the boys' new moves before they're used on an audience. Here I achieve the guaranteed-to-bring-the-house-down 'Retrieve the Saveloy with your Teeth' highlight to the first act - and on only my second attempt.
Poor Tony!

The dance step that had us in so much trouble with the Trades Description Act

Behind the scenes with...
JULIAN'S JOY BOYS

I personally vet all new members of my 'Joy Boys'

Stretching exercises are vital. This is just one of them

Before each show, we have a fifteen minute warm up session which involves all the dancers standing very close to me and reciting the names of quality fabrics. It does wonders for morale - and I think they quite enjoy it too

How to fo

Our 'Salute to James Anderton' always brings the house down.

Step three

Find the right performers

A likely candidate for your dance troupe

Chuck playing coy with the 'Retrieve the Saveloy number, after what happened to Tony.

n your own male dance troupe

Step two

Select just the right music to strip to

SUITABLE RECORDS TO STRIP TO
✔ Can You Feel The Force?
✔ Sex Machine
✔ I'm Too Sexy
✔ It's Raining Men

UNSUITABLE RECORDS TO STRIP TO
✘ Remember You're A Womble
✘ Away In A Manger
✘ BBC Radiophonic Workshop Sound Effects Record 2
✘ 'New World in the Morning' by Roger Whittaker

Russell

(I think that rather neatly says all that needs be said on this topic, don't you?)

JULIAN'S JOY BOYS SCANDAL

Manager fathered my triplets, says page 3 girl Kelly

'I don't think so,' says manager

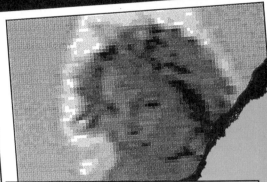

"WE'RE PULLING OUT!" SAY JOY BOYS

PANDEMONIUM hit Aylesbury yesterday when top male dancing troupe 'Julian's Joy Boys' cancelled last night's show at the Aylesbury Civic Centre.

Shoe shop girls and older married women from building societies were seen to be openly weeping in the streets.

"There simply wasn't enough baby oil and Heinz Salad Dressing in Aylesbury to cover every inch of the performers' muscular frames," explained Manager Julian Clary. "We felt the public would feel cheated if our hunks were not properly oiled and glistening - so we decided to cancel the show."

Attempts to airlift suitable quantities of oil and salad dressing are now underway from RAF Brize Norton in an attempt to save tonight's show.

Step four

Whip up the public's desire to see you by taking every opportunity for publicity

Step five

Go and play in all the dull, dreary towns full of bored housewives leading drab meaningless lives married to useless men. (Swindon is a good place to start)

THE REAL MAN AT WORK

THE FORMAL REAL MAN

DO YOU LIKE MY DICKIE?

THE BEST DRESSED REAL MAN

THE REAL MAN ON HOLIDAY

10 ITEMS OF CLOTHING A REAL MAN WILL NEVER ADMIT TO OWNING

1. Anything corduroy
2. Anything beige or pastel
3. Hush Puppies
4. A bright, fluffy alpaca jumper just like the ones that Russell Grant wears
5. A pair of red patent stilettos that just happen to be his size
6. Mittens
7. Jeans from M & S
8. A light blue safari suit
9. A beret
10. An anorak with fur-lined hood

HOW TO BE THE STRONG SILENT TYPE

(That's about it really)

AUSTRALIA
THE REAL MAN'S OWN COUNTRY

Time now, gentle reader, to put on your hiking slingbacks and follow me on an exploratory expedition down under.

They tell you that Australia is the land of opportunity - and I can personally vouch for that.

Australian men are such curious creatures, quintessential Real Men in all they think, do and say. And what a sporty bunch they are too! They excel at every ball game you can name.

TOURIST ATTRACTIONS OF AUSTRALIA

AYERS ROCK

(That's about it, really)

Now, you may have heard that Australians do not like us British, that they refer to us as whingeing poms - well, it's just not true! (I know - I had an assisted passage.) Australians love British men and you can always be sure of a warm reception in the outback, where complete strangers will share the contents of their tucker bag with you.

How did this strange breed of men develop? Perhaps it's not so surprising, when you think that they're descendants of British Real Men originally condemned to a life of penile servitude (which doesn't sound so bad to me, but they obviously saw it as a punishment back then).

THE FIVE MOST ELIGIBLE BACHELORS IN AUSTRALIA

1. Jason Donovan
2. Skippy
3. Farmer McDonald's prize bull, Bonker
4. Mel Gibson's brother, Fred
5. Craig McLaughlin's sister, Dave

BONDI BEACH
HOME OF THE REALEST MEN IN AUSTRALIA

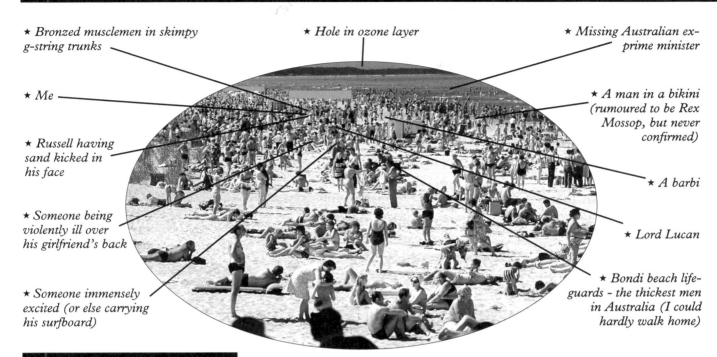

★ *Bronzed musclemen in skimpy g-string trunks*

★ *Me*

★ *Russell having sand kicked in his face*

★ *Someone being violently ill over his girlfriend's back*

★ *Someone immensely excited (or else carrying his surfboard)*

★ *Hole in ozone layer*

★ *Missing Australian ex-prime minister*

★ *A man in a bikini (rumoured to be Rex Mossop, but never confirmed)*

★ *A barbi*

★ *Lord Lucan*

★ *Bondi beach life-guards - the thickest men in Australia (I could hardly walk home)*

SIGNIFICANT MOMENTS IN AUSTRALIAN HISTORY

28 April 1770 - Captain Cook discovers Australia and lands at Botany Bay

(That's about it, really)

GREAT AUSTRALIAN CONTRIBUTIONS TO THE ENGLISH LANGUAGE

● **CHUNDER** - to be sick
● **KYLIE** - also to be sick (Derivation: 'I've produced a Kylie album')
● **WOBBLE BOARD** - a useless musical instrument
● **JASON** - to be severely, painfully heterosexual (as in 'Sorry, cobber, but I'm Jason!')
● **DIDGERY-DOO** - to be severely, joyfully homosexual
● **DONOVAN** - sexual inter-course between members of the opposite sex (as in 'Strewth! I could really give her a Donovan!')
● **J.D.** - truly masculine (as in 'My boyfriend Bruce is so J.D.!')

Advertising for Real Men

I'd do it if I thought it would work ...

Has someone been pulling your pilsner?

(Mine is red raw)

ADVERTISING FOR REAL MEN

YORKIE
BECAUSE IT GETS SO LONELY ON THOSE LONG DISTANCE DRIVES

FUN OUTINGS WITH THE LADS
THE PARK

NO BALL GAMES

NOT MY IDEA OF A FUN OUTING, I THINK WE'LL MOVE SWIFTLY ON, SHALL WE?

Things a Real Man will never admit to-

★ Secretly wanting to be on *Sticky Moments*
★ Having secretly appeared on *Sticky Moments*
★ Doing unnatural things with root vegetables while the wife's at Keep Fit
★ Being teetotal
★ Feeling cold on a building site
★ Not having had an erection since 1983

PLUMBER

'THE ~~WALRUS~~ AND THE CARPENTER'

The Plumber and the Carpenter
Were talking about work
They had a kitchen to install
For some old stupid berk
They thought about the tricks they'd play
Then they began to smirk.

'The time has come,' the Plumber said,
'To tell some whopping lies,
'The glue, the paint, the copper pipes
'We didn't really buy.
'It's all these "extras" added up
That make the cost so high.'

Soon the bill reached a thousand pounds
Then went up every day.
Next it doubled, then it trebled,

It wouldn't go away.
The householders had no idea
Of what they'd finally pay.

The delicate varnish finish
Was put on with a slap,
Both the plumbing and the drainage
Well, they weren't fit for scrap,
It met all their usual standards,
This kitchen that was crap.

The job was done and cash changed hands
The tradesmen said, 'That's it!'
They didn't bother clearing up
Before they both did split.
The Plumber and the Carpenter
- They didn't give a sh★t.

Bouncers in the mist

I DON'T wish to boast, but I am seldom refused entry, which is very pleasing, and I have yet to be ejaculated from a club by the bouncers. In fact, I believe that nightclub bouncers are sadly misunderstood creatures. Far from being the violent, dangerous animals that films like *King Kong* and *Conquest of the Planet of the Apes* have portrayed them to be, they are in fact shy, retiring and even timid creatures, only fierce when provoked.

So, as part of my research for this book, I set off, determined to live amongst wild bouncers for a while, to observe them at close quarters.

Hairy digits

After a tortuous journey fraught with danger up the Piccadilly Line, my native guide and I finally arrived at London's West End, where the biggest concentration of these magnificent animals still live in significant numbers.

I smelled them before I saw them (as far away as Acton Town tube), but after arriving at Leicester Square and turning a corner, I could hardly believe my eyes. There they were, Britain's largest mammals, milling around in significant numbers, grooming each other for fleas and nesting in the cave-like

Almost human! The doorman at Groucho's, Milton Keynes.

club entranceways. Immediately, I made to approach them.

'Any last minute advice?' I asked my guide.

'Yes. Approach them confidently, but be careful not to look them straight in the eye for too long. Don't sway, or give any other indication that you're drunk. And don't show any fear, whatever you do.'

Wear this badge with pride the next time you visit a night club

I'd only had two Babychams but I let it pass and I cautiously inched my way towards the 'flange' of bouncers lining the street - and suddenly found myself face to face with Keith, a big male 'Silverback' powerful enough to pull both your arms off (as he had done to one unfortunate who tried to enter his territory with brown shoes just the night before).

He looked me over with eyes that seemed to possess almost a human quality and sniffed the air, perhaps checking for concealed alcohol or

Boots aftershave. Then, ever so gently, he began to examine me with his rough, powerful hairy digits. At first I thought it was just curiosity - I'm used to that - then a thrill ran through me! I had made contact. I was being considered for inclusion.

Tentatively, I reached out to tickle his tummy. It was a heart-stopping moment - especially since all his mates were watching. Had I been accepted? I had! Keith rolled over on to his back and allowed me to pet him.

Wonderful beasts

It was a moment of pure magic. Here, on the edge of Leicester Square, I had made physical contact with a dim and distant relative of my species.

I will never forget my encounter with the bouncers of the West End, and so now I want to set the record straight on their fearsome reputation. They are wonderful beasts and we should do everything we can to preserve them.

WHAT TO DO IF YOU ARE APPROACHED BY A BOUNCER

1. **DO NOT RUN. Stand perfectly still.**
2. **Keep quiet. Do not provoke it by saying 'We're a coach party of sixteen lads down from Luton for the night' or 'Wanna buy a tab of E?'**
3. **If the bouncer starts to show signs of hostility, back off, eyes lowered, head bowed, murmuring soft, soothing words like 'Yeah, alright mate. We're on our way. No problem, eh?'**
4. **Bouncers are fiercely territorial. Do not provoke them by saying 'I didn't want to come into your miserable club anyway'.**
5. **If a bouncer starts to run its hands all over you, stand perfectly still and let it. This is part of a grooming ritual known as 'frisking', to ensure you present no threat. (It may also be a prelude to complimentary hand relief. Just stand back and think of Sigourney Weaver.)**

Wildlife in Danger

While they are not hunted by poachers, they do have a host of natural enemies, including the police, the DSS and the psychiatric review board. Many are captured and will spend the rest of their lives behind bars. With these sorts of problems, bouncers will need considerable resources devoted to them if they are to make it to the twenty first century.

HOW YOU CAN HELP TO PRESERVE THE BOUNCER
Start fights in nightclubs

Beauty and the Beast - I make friends with Stan at the Buccaneer Club, Old Compton Street

DOING TIME

Being sent to prison terrifies me. It's the thought of being banged up by some doddery old judge and then spending five to ten years with 200 hardened criminals. I think, however, that Real Men would never be frightened of committing crimes and being sent down. One of my recurring nightmares is that I'm trapped in a prison where most of the inmates are serving life for bad acting. That's right. In my dream I'm a PRISONER in CELL BLOCK H.

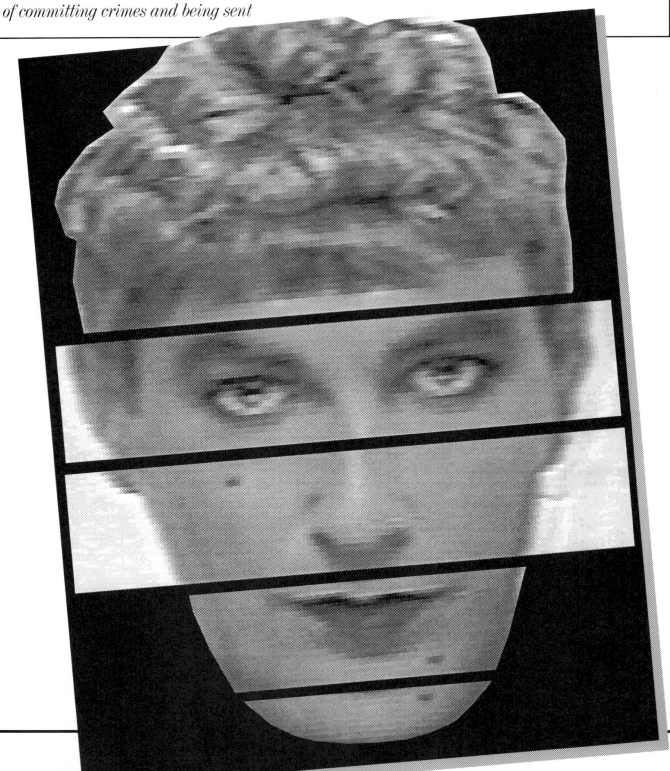

THE PLACE: Cell Block H
THE SENTENCE: Life
THE CRIME: Impersonating an actor and first degree murder of a script (you claim it was in self defence)

MY CELLMATE: I can't stand it any longer! I've been here for five years, locked up without a man and I'm desperate!

JULIAN: Calm yourself. Just imagine you're Debbie McGee, married to Paul Daniels. You'd be grateful you were under lock and key

MY CELLMATE: If I'm not locked in my cell I'm working in the laundry room

JULIAN: Well, I could think of a lot worse than handling peoples'smalls all day

MY CELLMATE: It's no good. I'm going to break out!

JULIAN: I know. I blame the prison food. It plays havoc with my skin tones

MY CELLMATE: No. I mean I've got to escape. I've been working on a plan for ages. Are you in?

JULIAN: Goodness. It's a long time since I've heard that expression

MY CELLMATE: I've found a passage I never knew existed

JULIAN (BREATHLESS): Do tell!

MY CELLMATE: If we crawl through the ventilation ducts we can reach the Governor's office and take him by surprise

JULIAN: That's often the best way, but isn't it a bit reckless?

MY CELLMATE: I don't care, I'm in for a long stretch

JULIAN: It's not the D-Wing enema competition is it?

MY CELLMATE: I carved this fake gun out of soap so we can hold the Governor hostage. Do you think it's convincing?

JULIAN: Well. It no longer looks like anything I've ever seen in the showers. I'll say no more

MY CELLMATE: We'll have to be quick. You know about the random strip searches here where they check you're not concealing a weapon

JULIAN: Pinch me, I'm dreaming!

GOOD CRIMES TO GO TO PRISON FOR

- ✔ Murder
- ✔ Manslaughter
- ✔ Aggravated assault
- ✔ Grievous wounding
- ✔ Assault with a deadly weapon
- ✔ Extortion with menaces
- ✔ Impersonating a police officer
- ✔ Anything involving firearms

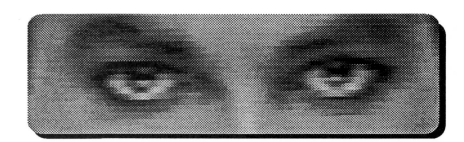

BAD CRIMES TO GO TO PRISON FOR

- ✘ Being found in the Queen Mother's bedroom
- ✘ Anything involving marsupials
- ✘ Robbing people's houses while they're in jail
- ✘ Desecrating the Krays' mum's grave
- ✘ Not buying a TV licence
- ✘ Fouling a public footpath
- ✘ Breaking windows
- ✘ Nothing

ADVANTAGES OF GOING TO PRISON FOR 25 YEARS TO LIFE

- ✔ You'll never have to buy a round
- ✔ You'll only have to see your wife once a week
- ✔ She'll never find out if you're cheating on her
- ✔ You won't have to pay your poll tax
- ✔ You'll get all your meals free
- ✔ You won't need to bother deciding what to wear
- ✔ You won't have to stagger home blind drunk after a night out with the lads
- ✔ All your mates are there
- ✔ You'll be able to have sex any night you want
- ✔ No one need know about your secret homosexual yearnings

DISADVANTAGES OF GETTING A 25 YEARS TO LIFE SENTENCE

By the time you're released:
- ✘ Beer will be £18.20 a Euro-pint
- ✘ Your football team will be relegated to the Vauxhall Beazer Homes Queensway Asda Superstore Conference League (Division 3 - South)
- ✘ You'll look like Reg Varney
- ✘ Your wife/girlfriend will also look like Reg Varney
- ✘ Your application for a council flat will still not have reached the top of the list
- ✘ Everything you know about plumbing will be out of date
- ✘ Your secret homosexual yearnings will have been well and truly satisfied

HOW TO ESCAPE

And if you do go to prison and you decide it's really not for you, well, who could blame you? The best way to escape is to have a close friend bake you a cake with a file hidden in it. It's an old trick but it just might work. My friend Victor is a very well-known pastry chef- in fact he's a self-raising man. Here's his recipe for Coconut Cake. Marvellous.

COCONUT CAKE

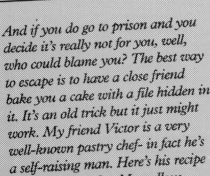

Ingredients:

1 file
175g butter or margarine
175g sugar
3 eggs
225g self-raising flour
75g dessicated coconut
pinch of salt
2 tablespoons milk
4 tablespoons jam
caster sugar to sprinkle

METHOD

Cream the butter and sugar together
Add the eggs one at a time, beating well
Fold in the flour, coconut and salt with the milk
Turn the mixture into a greased 20cm cake tin
Bake in a moderate oven (180 degrees C, Gas Mark 4) for 30 minutes
Turn the cake out to cool
When cold, split into two layers
Insert the file and sandwich together with the jam
Sprinkle with caster sugar and coconut

Note:
These are the wrong types of files:
* *Lever-arch file*
* *Nail file*

GOOD JOBS FOR REAL MEN

HUNK

It's a fair cop - or at least one with highlights! PC Julian says he'd like to take you down to the station - or anywhere else really - and judging by the size of his truncheon, you'd be lucky to come quietly. With Julian on the beat it's a pleasure to be caught by the fuzz.

KING OF THE ROAD

HOW MOST MEN BUY A CAR:

SALESMAN: Good morning, sir. Can I help you?

MOST MEN: I'm interested in this four-door model. What's the on-the-road price?

SALESMAN: That will be £10,650 sir.

MOST MEN: OK.What about consumption? Does it take unleaded petrol?

SALESMAN: Yes, and it's got a special lean-burn engine that gives about 32mpg in town.

MOST MEN: I see. What size engine is that?

SALESMAN: It's a sixteen-valve 1.5 litre with catalytic converter.

MOST MEN: And it comes with a year's warranty?

SALESMAN: That's right, sir, and a...

(CONTINUES FOR ANOTHER 47 MINUTES WITH QUESTIONS ABOUT SAFETY, DELIVERY, OPTIONS FOR VELOUR UPHOLSTERY, THE SUNROOF, SERVICING INTERVALS, MUD FLAPS, METALLIC PAINT ETC.,ETC.,)

BUYING A CAR

When it comes to cars I'm one of those people who doesn't know his big end from his thrust bearing - although I know a man who does. Now, most men go through a particular routine when it comes to buying a car. They're quite sensible about it and asks loads of relevant questions. The Real Man, on the other hand, can't be bothered with all that nonsense...

HOW A REAL MAN BUYS A CAR:

REAL MAN: Watcha mate! This one's a bit tasty. How loud's the stereo then?

SALESMAN: Well, sir, it's got a 200-watt power amplifier and...

REAL MAN: I'll bleedin' take it!

HOW JULIAN BUYS A CAR:

JULIAN: Have you got something nice in blue with a big rear view mirror?

IDENTIFYING ROAD SIGNS

Tits out for the lads!	
Inebriated motorist ahead	
Extremely inebriated motorist ahead	
Lavvy	**P**
Dodgy kebab shop	
Tony's wife	
Moving target	
Run over a cat	
Time to call in the Trades Descriptions Act?	
Route home from the pub	

THE REAL HARD MAN

You can't get much harder than the men in the SAS. They're ever so tough. They're trained to withstand terrible torture, like having their fingernails ripped out one by one. Just imagine having that done when you've just had a manicure. What a dreadful waste of acrylic glaze.

They also have to learn advanced unarmed combat, like how to kill a man using just your little finger... actually, I think I might know how that's done, but you'd need a pair of Marigolds. The thing I like most about the SAS is their fashion sense. Deep, dark colours really suit a masculine build.

Black is back! ▶

Dressed to kill with the SAS! It's moody. It's mysterious. It's marvellous.
- The SAS Winter '92 Combat Collection.

Things a Real Man will never admit to

★ Finding pornography offensive

★ Loving someone (except his Rottweiler)

★ Ever being rejected by a girl

★ Painting his nails with a red felt pen just to see what they'd look like

Machine gun: Model's own

Optional bobble-hat. Stunningly simple. Fuller pom-poms are now back in vogue for that vibrant, masculine look. Sizes 3 1/4 - 11 1/2 (£12, Army & Navy)

Balaclava. Elegantly styled with a deep aperture for maximum field of vision. 60% wool. Sizes S, M, L (£6 - £9, Army & Navy)

Pure alpaca wool. Tapered at the waist for that subtle variation on a theme. With or without leather elbow reinforcing patches. Chests 36" - 48" (£64, Army & Navy)

Dyed pigskin with stainless buckle. The essential accessory. Suits waists 30" to 44" (£22, Army & Navy)

For versatility these cotton fatigues have been tailored so they can be worn tucked in or out of boots. Waists 30" to 40" (£42, Army & Navy)

Classically styled 12-hole combat boots. Leather uppers with synthetic sole. Nice in patent leather. Sizes 5 - 12 (£56, Army & Navy)

THE MAGIC SENSUA

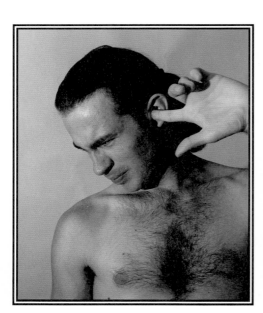

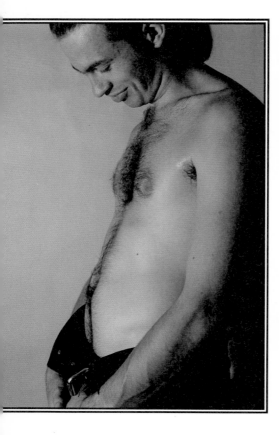

LITY *of* REAL MEN

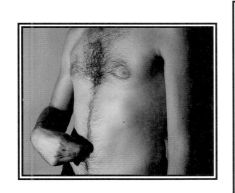

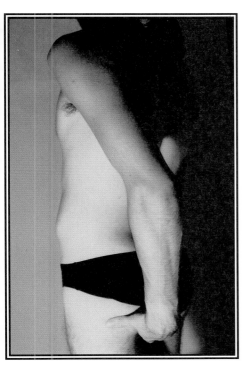

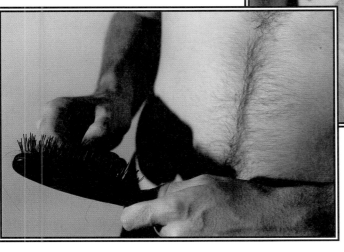

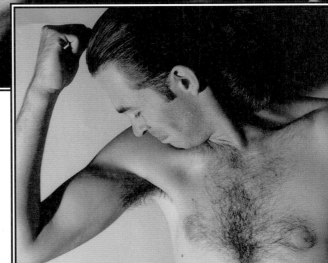

WORLD OF SPORTS

SOCCER

How much appeal can there be in a sport full of men who dribble before they shoot? What happened to proper ball control, that's what I want to know?

I had the misfortune to watch England recently. All those wasted balls and fumbled passes. I'm sure if I was placed on the England team, I'd score. In fact, they should make me the manager. I'd have the team working on their thrusts from the back for a start, and everyone would have to clean up their tackles.

(Mind you, I'd also like to see some changes made to the rules; I think 'handballs' should be positively encouraged.)

BOWLS

Not for the living.

BOXING

While I detest physical violence, you can't help but admire a man who knows how to use his fists in the ring.

POTHOLING

I really can't see why people are so interested in exploring some dark, damp hole. I mean, can you imagine being the first to go down, then squeezing yourself through the narrowest of openings, inch by inch, and wriggling about. Where's the appeal in that?

ROWING

What a graceful sport to watch! Eight men, all stroking in time, taking it from the cox, all straining to beat off the opposition and pulling frantically to the finish. The perfect sport for Oxford and Cambridge undergraduates, without any doubt.

SUMO

How horrid.

THE LONG JUMP

Chance would be a fine thing.

GOLF

What a disappointment! For years I've been in search of the legendary 'British Open' - and now I find it's not a window dresser from Islington after all, but just some old golf tournament...

BASKETBALL

Ahh! The sound of balls slapping against the rim. Music to my ears.

ICE HOCKEY

Lots of men sliding about and 80 mph pucks. Whatever happened to romance?

ONE-UPMANSHIP

Not officially a sport - which is a shame, because I'm sure I'd be very good at it.

JULIAN'S INFERNO
The Real Man's final destination

For all the earthly pleasures you'll receive when you become a Real Man (thanks to my guide) you have to pay a price.

Hell is the final destination of the Real Man's selfish and thoroughly corrupt soul, and you were irretrievably damned the moment you took your first piece of seemingly innocuous advice. But that's not the end of the bad news. There's worse to come. Because Hell is modelled on an English seaside resort - Bournemouth, to be precise - and you have to spend all eternity there.

A TOURIST GUIDE TO HELL

ROAD TO NOWHERE

PLEASURE GARDENS, HEAVING WITH BUBBLING BRIMSTONE

THE ONLY CINEMA IN HELL (SHOWING GLEN OR GLENDA, NOW HELD OVER FOR THE TENTH STRAIGHT CENTURY)

THE ONE PUB SERVING THE WHOLE OF HELL.

ZOMBIFIED SHAMBLING OLD PEOPLE TALKING ABOUT WRITING POSTCARDS

TOPLESS BEACH (OVER 70s ONLY)

BIG BEEFY LIFEGUARDS WHO ARE MORE THAN ANXIOUS TO GIVE YOU THE KISS OF LIFE, EVEN THOUGH YOU'VE BEEN NOWHERE NEAR THE SEA.

TERRY SCOTT AT THE END OF THE PIER UNTIL ETERNITY

SEA OF PURE FIRE

ICE CREAM STALL, CLOSED, WITH A NOTICE SAYING 'BACK IN 10 EONS'

N

200 m

CANS OF WARM PANDA COLA THAT COST EXACTLY TEN TIMES WHAT YOU HAVE IN YOUR POCKET (AND TWENTY TIMES WHAT YOU IMAGINED THEY'D COST)

THE SPINNERS IN CONCERT AT THE PAVILION

PERSONAL APPEARANCE BY THE DALLAS COWBOY CHEERLEADERS, CANCELLED EVERY TEN MINUTES UNTIL THE END OF TIME

HELL FOR DOUBLE-JOINTED BAD GIRLS WITH BIG BREASTS AND NO MORALS, SEPARATED FROM YOU FOR ALL ETERNITY BY AN IMPASSABLE RAVINE OF EVERLAST-ING FIRE, LAVA AND NELSON EDDY SONGS

PROMENADE LAND TRAIN, WHICH THE REALLY DAMNED SOULS HAVE TO RIDE ON FOR ALL ETERNITY, CONDEMNED TO WAVE FURIOUSLY AND CALL 'COO-EE' TO PASSERS-BY

THE ONLY PUB IN HELL

The Real Man's final destination

Sooner or later, every Real Man ends up here.

Passing inside, you find that the walls are tastefully decorated with old horsebrasses and even older looking framed cigarette cards which, on closer inspection, depict 'Opportunities You Missed During Your Life', 'Women Who Rejected You During Your Lifetime' and 'Blokes Your Girlfriend Was Sleeping With Behind Your Back' (collect all 580 cards in the set). The cigarette machine only takes Djibouti 5-Franc coins and, anyway, has nothing in it but the worst cigarettes you ever bought in Spain. The video game is 'Pong', but there's a 10,000-year wait to get on it and it's broken anyway.

When you finally struggle through the crowd and reach the bar, a process taking roughly as long again as the rise of civilisation, all the barmen look like Robert Maxwell - as do all the barmaids. The only beer being served at the bar is Kaliber, but it's so crowded and infernally hot in the pub that you'll even drink that. Attracting the attention of the bar staff takes in the region of twenty years - more on Saturdays. However, every time you finally succeed in buying a pint, someone spills it for you. This goes on for until you finally give up or resort to sucking the beer-soaked flannels (something I tried in my youth at Henley Royal Regatta - it can be surprisingly satisfying).

The entertainment in the pub is Karaoke - which would be fine for you, except a party of Swiss-German Real Men are hogging the microphone and singing a flat, heavily accented version of 'Nights in White Satin'.

At the other end of the pub you find the jukebox. This provides no refuge, because the jukebox is packed with Brotherhood of Man B-Sides and old Eurovision hits - and someone has elected to play nothing but the Swedish 1984 entry - 'Diggi Loo - Diggi Ley' - for the rest of time.

And that's just the start of your torments. All the attractive women are with boyfriends eight feet tall with low, jutting foreheads who eat nothing but pint glasses, everyone's heard all your jokes, no-one knows where the loos are and someone is always being sick on your back.

And, worst of all, all your old chums are there and desperately on the pull - while you've been reincarnated as a tall blonde girl in a skimpy white dress who looks like she might have been stood up. Imagine being asked if you're a model for all eternity. Hahahahahaha hahahahaha haha haha!

Serves you right for being a Real Man.

Other books by Julian Clary

*The Joan Collins Fan Club:
My Life With Fanny The
Wonder Dog (with Paul
Merton)*

Other books by
Mark Leigh & Mike Lepine

The Complete Revenge Kit
*How To Be A Complete Bastard
(with Adrian Edmondson)*
*How To Be A Complete Bitch (with
Pamela Stephenson)*
The Book Of Revelations
The Naughty 90s
*The Return Of The Complete
Revenge Kit*
How To Be A Superhero
The Book Of Stupid Lists

Costumes created by

MICHAEL FERRI

Acknowledgements

Thanks to the following Real Men
(and Women)

MAGNUS BOWDEN, KEITH BRAZIL,
SEAMUS CASSIDY, DAVID CHAPMAN,
JOHN CHOOPANI,
ADDISON CRESSWELL,
GRAHAM EAMES, CHRIS FORDWOH,
HARRIE GREEN, ANDI HAMMERSON,
PHILIPPA HATTON,
SALLY HOLLOWAY, IN STITCHES
(WEALDSTONE), ADAM LEIGH,
DEBBIE LEIGH, POLLY LEIGH,
KARIN LEITE, SHAUN LESTER,
JOHN MARKHAM, JERRY MASON,
IMOGEN PARKER, BILL PAYNE,
CHRIS PHILLIPS, POET'S CORNER,
(BOURNEMOUTH), SHARON ROSE,
JANE SCARROW, ROB SHREEVE,
JULIE SMITH, STOCKPILE,
KATE STRONG (MAKE-UP),
PATRICK O'SULLIVAN'S PUB,
(FULHAM), TIM TAYLOR,
TRACY WHEELER, THE WORX . . .
AND I SUPPOSE, RUSSELL CHURNEY